MW01601688

The Green Print
The Sativa Certification Program
An Interactive Master Course to Cannabis

In order to gain access to your interactive online cannabis training that is included with this book 100% free, please visit www.learnsativa.org/book-training.

Place training product in your cart & use coupon code "BOOK" to gain instant access.

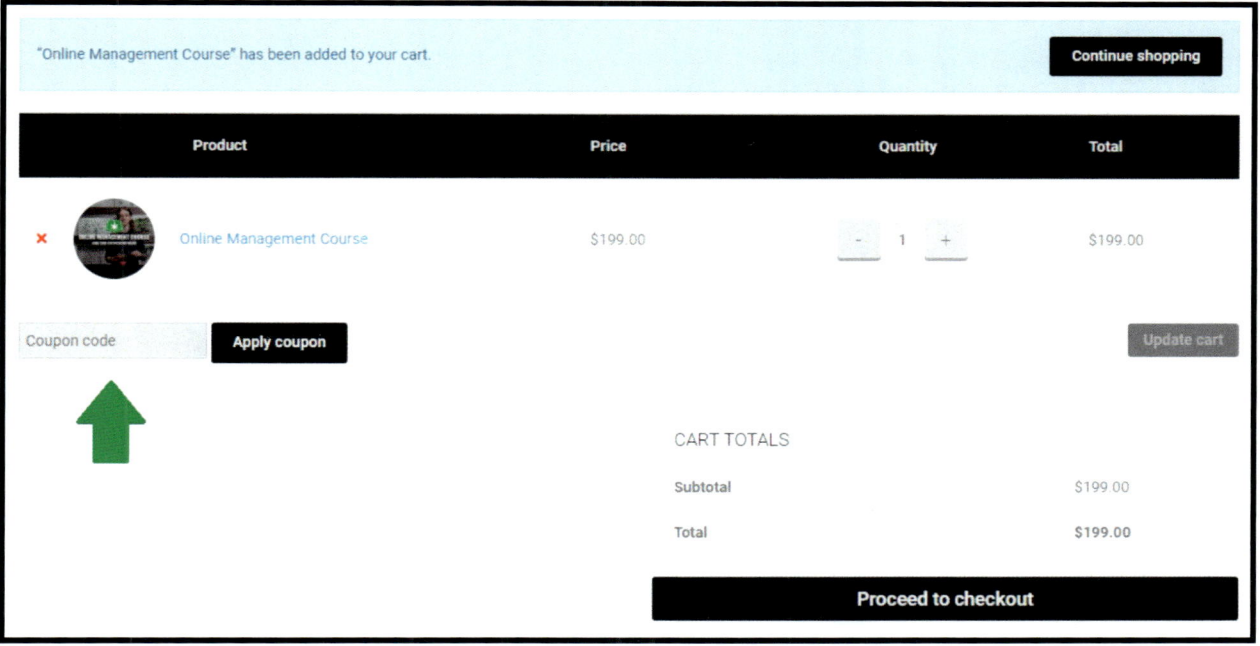

The Ultimate Cannabis Education Handbook

<u>A Message from the Author</u>

The Cannabis industry is *NOT* the "Gold Rush".

You want to make millions overnight and have somebody make unrealistic promises that you'll do so?

Then buy a Tai Lopez course.

Otherwise,

Allow me to welcome you to the <u>$52.5 billion</u> Cannabis industry.

The Gold Rush was based off of dumb luck. You bought a shovel, dug in the dirt forever for the sheer possibility of digging up a spec of gold.

The reason <u>I love this</u> industry is simple.

You can make great money, **while helping people.**

Roll up your sleeves, get your hands dirty and you will succeed in this industry - plain and simple.

It's not about luck here, it's about **<u>accountability</u>**.

And Remember, **Knowledge is Power.**

Patrick O'Brien
Founder & CEO of Learn Sativa University
Author of "The Green Print" & "The Two Pound Book"

Table of Contents...

Week One:
View Week One Lecture & Slides in Training Portal, then...
Jobs in the Cannabis Industry (Page 7)
Sativa vs Indica (Page 17)
Hemp vs Marijuana (Page 27)
Types of Cannabis (Page 39)

Week Two:
View Week Two Lecture & Slides in Training Portal, then...
What is the Endocannabinoid System (Page 47)
What Are Terpenes (Page 59)
The Entourage Effect (Page 63)
Predicting Your High from THC & CBD (Page 69)
Popular Cannabinoids & Effects (Page 79)

Week Three:
View Week Three Lecture & Slides in Training Portal, then...
Ingest or Inhale? (Page 91)
Concentrates vs Flower (Page 97)
Options for Consuming (Page 103)
What Affects Your High? (Page 111)
Counteracting Your High (Page 117)
Best Strains for Beginners (Page 123)
Microdosing (Page 129)

How to Grow Cannabis / The Right Way (Step-by-Step)
The Ultimate Grow Guide (Page 147)

Bonus Material 100% Free (Page 177)

Jobs in The Cannabis Industry...

There's no way around it: the cannabis industry is the fastest-growing sector in the United States - and jobs in the field are in *high* demand. If you're looking to pivot your career into a new, lucrative, and exciting realm of work, then jobs within the cannabis industry are ripe for picking. Read along to discover the wide range of positions within the cannabis industry - along with their associated yearly salary and unique perks.

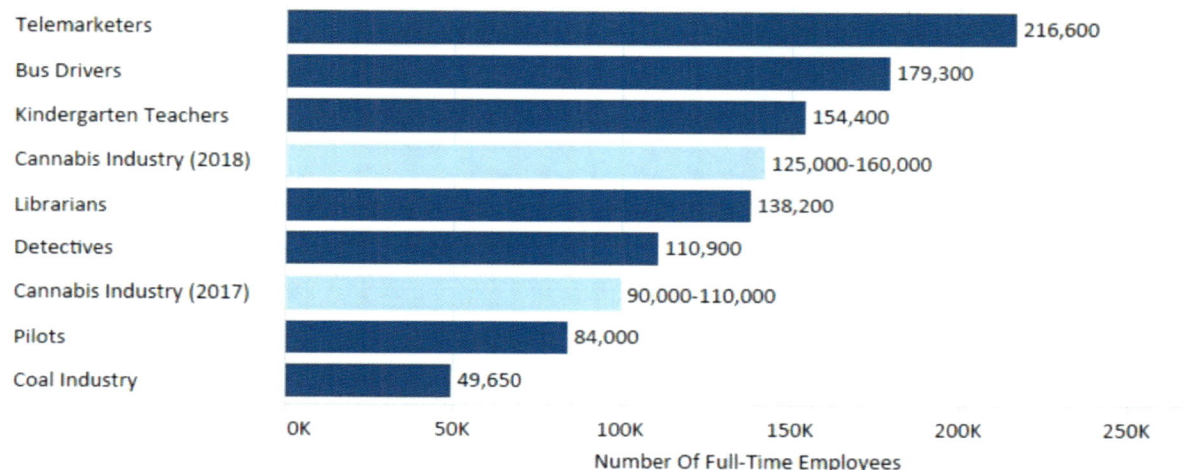

(Shown Above: Cannabis job growth chart. Photo Credits: Marijuana Business Daily)

Why Work In The Cannabis Industry?

This is a question that many of you have asked yourselves hundreds of times. Why work in an industry that still isn't recognized by the United States federal government? Federal law classifies cannabis that contains over 0.3% THC as a substance that's as dangerous as methamphetamine, cocaine, and heroin.

Although the federal government doesn't agree with the cannabis industry at large - they *will* come around to it. If you're still wondering *why* they'll eventually cave in, then one only needs to think about what makes the world go 'round. Money is the answer - and lots of it.

The cannabis industry in the US encompasses 33 states that have legalized medicinal or recreational cannabis. Many other states are rapidly succumbing to the domino effect, and it's only a matter of time until federal entities scratch their heads, wondering how they can get a piece of the pie.

California's legal cannabis industry accumulated over $300 million in tax revenue in 2018. Washington outdid itself and pulled even more than California, totaling $319 million in tax revenue. Colorado netted $266 million, Oregon made $94 million, Nevada amassed $70 million, Alaska raised $11 million, and Massachusetts tax revenue totaled $5 million.[1]

What do these numbers tell you? Of course, by just looking at them, they seem impressive. However, when compared with data from previous years (in Colorado), and estimates from revered business analysts, all signs point to a *booming* industry.

Currently, analysts are forecasting that the US cannabis industry is slated for over 24% in compound annual growth rate (CAGR).[2] This is unheard of growth in any other industry in the United States (or the world for that matter). As of 2018, the legal cannabis industry in the US was worth roughly $12 billion - all while being utterly *dwarfed* by black market marijuana operations.

Any state that's been hit with hard financial times sees cannabis as their guiding light out of the tunnel. The potential for stimulating economic growth by embracing the cannabis industry is too hard to pass up.

Now, the amount of money being spent on cannabis is astounding, and this is all made possible by the workers behind the scenes who keep the *green machine* alive and well. These workers are budtenders, plant scientists, chemists, pest management professionals, soil scientists, delivery drivers, dispensary managers, canna-chefs, bud trimmers, and many more.

---

[1]
https://www.forbes.com/sites/niallmccarthy/2019/03/26/which-states-made-the-most-tax-revenue-from-marijuana-in-2018-infographic/#5433a2707085
[2] https://www.grandviewresearch.com/press-release/global-legal-marijuana-market

Each of these roles is filled by individuals like you and me, and they are moving ahead of the trend to secure their position in our generation's most important commodity: cannabis.

The Demand For Cannabis Workers

The cannabis industry is the fastest-growing job-market because the numbers say so. In 2018 alone, over 60,000 jobs were added to the cannabis industry in the United States. The total number of estimated jobs in the cannabis field is over 200,000. If we're too include periphery services, then the total number would be nearly 300,000.[3]

Although jobs are being cut in other fields due to a slowing nationwide economy, the cannabis industry is doing the exact opposite. Ranks in the cannabis industry are quickly being bolstered as many individuals see the marijuana field as their ticket to a successful career in a lucrative industry.

The demand for cannabis workers is unlikely to slow down as many states are preparing their own legal framework for medicinal or recreational cannabis. As new states introduce cannabis into their own economies, jobs are expected to spike.

Overall, the jobs within cannabis are not ephemeral, as some skeptics may claim. Instead, jobs within the marijuana industry have the potential to come with benefit packages, such as healthcare, dental, insurance, vacation time, and other perks.

Jobs Within The Cannabis Industry

Now, let's take a look at some of the most popular jobs within the cannabis industry.

Canna-Chef

This newly coined position is for those that have culinary expertise. The job entails a wide variety of options for those that are adept at creating foodie masterpieces - all while adding just the right amount of cannabis to the mix.

---

[3]

https://www.cnbc.com/2019/03/14/the-marijuana-industry-looks-like-the-fastest-growing-job-market-in-the-country.html

The most in-demand position in a cannabis kitchen is that of a head chef. This position demands a chef who's accustomed to a high-pace workplace that can command the respect of his or her workers.

(Shown Right: Cannabis Edibles make up 60% of the industry. Photo Credits: Leafly)

These positions are meant for oversight of an entire cannabis-infused edible production line. A head chef's salary can reach upwards of $90,000 per year.

An up-and-coming position that's guaranteed to pay big is a read-deal canna-chef at upcoming marijuana cafes. California is the first state to allow such an operation, and they will resemble what the dutch have had for years - a business that allows the sale and consumption of cannabis-based products on site. Canna-chefs that work in these few establishments can make clear over $100,000 per year.

If you're new to the culinary field, then you can secure an entry-level job working as a line cook, dishwasher, or cook. These entry-level positions can net you between $20,000-40,000 per year.

Budtender

The budtender is the face of a licensed cannabis dispensary. These individuals are responsible for ensuring that patrons get *exactly* what they want. If a customer is on the hunt of a strain that smells like pineapples and makes them energetic - then it's the budtender's job to find this variety.

(Shown Above: Inside look of a dispensary. Photo Credits: Cova Software)

Budtenders are the unsung heroes of the cannabis industry because they answer questions, day in and day out, without asking for a mere thank you. This position requires in-depth knowledge of everything-cannabis. Strains, effects, medicinal properties, and knowledge of health issues are key when studying to become a budtender.

The budtender pays $13-17 per hour or roughly $30,000 per year.[4] As the cannabis market becomes more specialized and competitive, it's probable that this position's wage will increase.

Master Grower

The master grower position is the highest rank that any cultivator can achieve. This position is only meant for highly experienced individuals that have been at the helm of large scale operations. This job entails the management of thousands of plants that are at different stages of life. Seedlings, clones, vegetative stage,

flowering phase; along with the subsequent harvest and post-harvest process.

(Shown Above: A cannabis grow technician tending plants. Photo Credits: The Australian)

The scope of a master grower is extensive; however, the rewards are massive. According to Monster, master growers can make upwards of $100,000. This six-figure position is heavily sought after - therefore, you must be ready to stand out amongst a sea of other qualified individuals.

---

[4] https://www.payscale.com/research/US/Job=Budtender/Hourly_Rate

Extraction Technician

Cannabis extracts are some of the hottest products in the marijuana market. These potent and flavorful concentrates have become the centerpiece of the cannabis community, and those who produce them are highly regarded.

(Shown Left: Extract tech holding top quality product.)

This position was held by individuals without any prior lab experience before legalization. However, the legalization of cannabis has pushed for adequate experience as a lab technician to qualify for this role.

Extraction technicians are exposed to many potentially dangerous chemicals during the production of cannabis concentrates. Due to this, there are many protocols in place that require workers and employers to have adequate training with various compounds and extraction techniques.

Extraction technicians can expect to net $20,000-40,000 per year.[5] It'll be expected of you to hold a bachelor's degree at a minimum, or a master's degree in engineering, chemistry, or biology.

Extraction Leader

An extraction leader is responsible for making an entire marijuana concentrate operation *flow*. This means that they are a person who tells extraction technicians what to do - and how to do it. This role is a leadership role, which means that you'll have to oversee the production of cannabis concentrates, the safety of your workers, and the protocols in place.

This is a high-stress position because cannabis extraction labs are filled with many hazardous materials. However, if you hold a Ph.D. in physics, chemistry, biology, or

---

5

https://www.monster.com/career-advice/article/booming-legal-marijuana-industry-has-jobs-that-pay-50k-to-90k

engineering with prior experience in a laboratory, then this position may be just right for you.

Extraction leaders can expect to make over $100,000. This is a guaranteed six-figure position and can be incredibly lucrative when working with large-scale facilities.

(Shown Above: Patrick and Doctor Byron performing an extraction in the Advanced extraction course.)

Dispensary Manager

The dispensary manager position is meant for individuals who are ready to guide a cannabis retail store towards success. Dispensary managers are responsible for the employees, their tasks, and the overall function of the entire business.

(Shown Above: Thomas standing in as a potential dispensary manager.)

This job entails a large amount of responsibility because dispensary managers also work with vendors, law enforcement, customers, and the training of new employees. The day-to-day operations fall on the shoulders of the dispensary manager, which means you'll need the mental and physical strength of the titan Atlas.

If you have previous managerial experience in a high-paced environment, then working as a dispensary manager may be just right for you. This position can pay between $60,000-150,000 per year. Depending on the dispensary, you should also expect a broad range of benefits - from insurance to vacation time.

Cultivator

The cannabis cultivator is an essential position within the cannabis industry. These individuals are responsible for keeping cannabis plants at all stages of life alive.

(Shown Left: Cannabis Tech's in action.)

Without adequate cultivators, the production of marijuana products would quickly cease, and the overall quality would decline rapidly.

Although master growers are responsible for the entire operation at hand, cultivators do daily tasks such as watering, feeding, pruning, cloning, transplanting, IPM, soil management, and much more. Cultivators are tasked with many crucial responsibilities, and because of this, are some of the most in-demand individuals in the cannabis job market.

For a cultivator position, it's recommended that you have the prior horticultural experience, such as working in a nursery or garden. Although a bachelor's degree isn't a requirement, it would significantly help your chances.

This position has an average base pay of $15 or roughly $30,000 per year.

Trimmer

When customers admire the cannabis in their hand, they are marveling at the work of bud trimmers. Although master growers and cultivators are responsible for the flowers - the trimmers are responsible for the end product.

(Shown Right: A trimmer preparing to harvest their crops.)

Trimmers manicure each flower after harvest and again after the initial drying session. Being a trimmer isn't easy work because it requires you to understand the bud structure of Sativas, Indicas, and Hybrids. Each of the cannabis types has different characteristics, such as the high-density of Indica flowers and the fluffier style of Sativas.

This position also requires workers to sit for hours on end and trim small leaves off of flowers. Prior experience isn't necessarily required for this position. The pay for bud trimmers is roughly $12-18 per hour or $20,000 per-year.

However, this job is commonly viewed as seasonal work - primarily when the cannabis is grown outdoors. If cannabis is produced indoors, then this position can be year round.

Which Job is Right For You?

If you're ready to join the ranks of the cannabis industry - then there's no better time than now. The momentum is growing, and it's recommended to get your foot in the door before the cannabis sector becomes truly mainstream.

Whether you're looking for a managerial position or an entry-level job, the cannabis industry has something for everyone. It wasn't too long ago that countless individuals that are a part of the growing marijuana industry picked up everything and relocated halfway across the nation. Now, with so many states giving the green light to medicinal or recreational cannabis, job seekers won't have to travel so far to become a part of the booming marijuana industry.

POP QUIZ

Question #1: What's the highest paying career in the cannabis industry?

Answer: _____

Question #2: Who is responsible for overseeing the production of cannabis concentrates, the safety of your workers, and the protocols put in place?

Answer: _____

Question #3: This job entails the management of thousands of plants that are at different stages of life. Seedlings, clones, vegetative stage, flowering phase; along with the subsequent harvest and post-harvest process.

Answer: _____

Sativa vs. Indica: An Overview of Cannabis Types...

If you've ever walked through a marijuana dispensary, then you've likely seen the endless array of cannabis strains. Usually, each strain has information regarding its lineage, such as its parents and its classification as a sativa or indica. By understanding what a sativa or indica *is*, then you'll have a much easier time picking which strain is best for you.

Read along to understand the unique characteristics that separate indicas and sativas - and why it should matter to you.

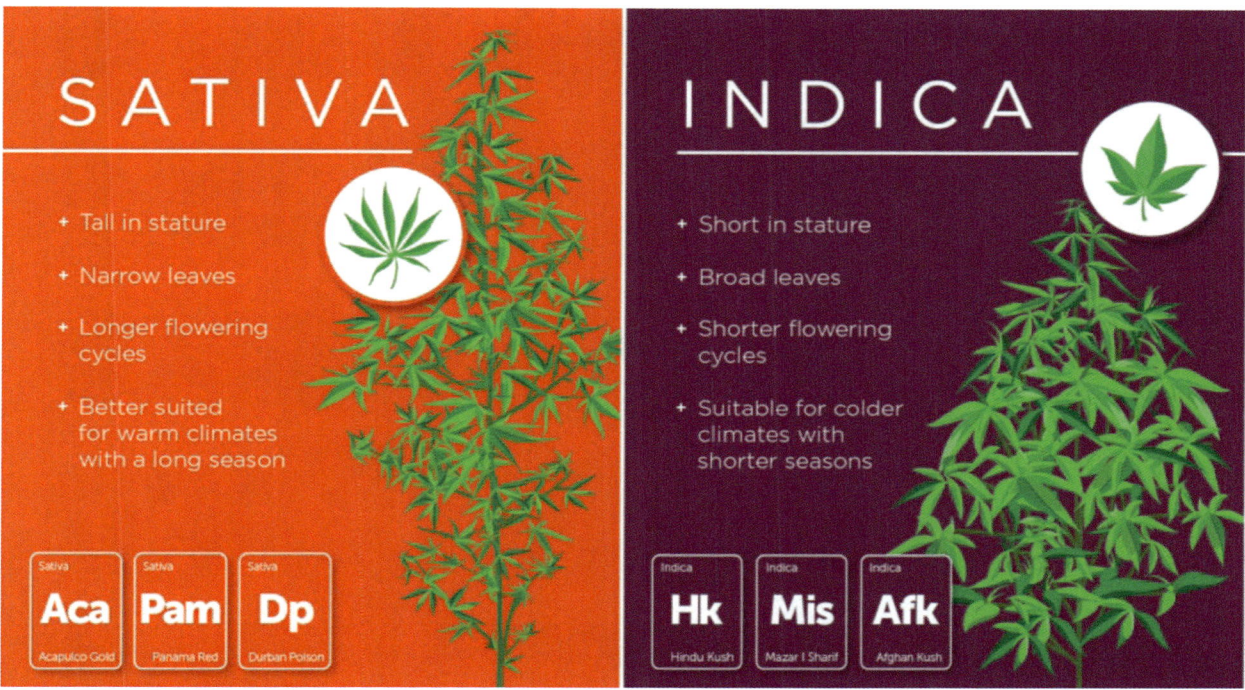

(Shown Above: Sativa vs Indica chart. Photo Credits: Leafly)

Terpenes And Their Role in *Cannabis indica* and *sativa*

Before we delve into the differences between indica and sativa, we should describe the influence that terpenes play in each cannabis variety. It's recently been discovered that terpenes play a significant role in the effects we feel after consuming sativa or indica strains.

GUIDE TO TERPENES

	Aroma	Vaporizes at	Found in	Strains		
PNE α-PINENE	Pine	311°F (155°C)	Pine Needles, Rosemary, Basil, Parsley, Dill	**Pk** Indica Purple Kush	**Bay** Sativa Bay Dream	**Ak** Hybrid AK-47
MYR MYRCENE	Cloves Earthy Herbal	332°F (167°C)	Mango, Lemongrass, Thyme, Hops	**Gdp** Indica Granddaddy Purple	**Am** Sativa Amnesia	**Tw** Hybrid Trainwreck
LME LIMONENE	Citrus	348°F (176°C)	Fruit Rinds, Rosemary, Juniper, Peppermint	**Hk** Indica Hindu Kush	**Lmg** Sativa Lemon G	**Stb** Hybrid Strawberry Banana
CYE CARYOPHYLLENE	Pepper Spicy Woody Cloves	266°F (130°C)	Black Pepper, Cloves, Cinnamon	**Fog** Hybrid Fire OG	**Gg4** Hybrid GG4	**Gsc** Hybrid GSC
LNL LINALOOL	Floral	388°F (198°C)	Lavender	**Kos** Indica Kosher Kush	**Rom** Indica Romulan	**Sk** Hybrid Sour Kush
HUM HUMULENE	Woody Earthy	222°F (106°C)	Hops, Coriander, Cloves, Basil	**Bcg** Indica Black Cherry OG	**Ds** Indica Death Star	**Gsc** Hybrid GSC
OCM OCIMENE	Sweet Herbal Woody	122°F (50°C)	Mint, Parsley, Pepper, Basil, Mangoes, Orchids, Kumquats	**Sen** Indica Sensi Star	**Dp** Sativa Durban Poison	**Svb** Hybrid Silver Bubble
TPE TERPINOLENE	Pine Floral Herbal	366°F (186°C)	Nutmeg, Tea Tree, Conifers, Apples, Cumin, Lilacs	**Dt** Hybrid Dutch Treat	**Gth** Sativa Ghost Train Haze	**Ago** Hybrid Agent Orange

(Shown Above: Terpenes chart. Photo Credits: Leafly)

Terpenes are organic compounds that are found throughout the plant kingdom. They're responsible for the aroma and taste of various flowers, fruits, and plant structures. For instance, can you guess what smell is associated with the terpene limonene? If you guess lemons, then you're correct. There are over 20,000 terpenes in existence, and 100 of them can be found throughout cannabis varieties.

Researchers believe that terpenes can influence cannabinoids, as well as create medicinal effects of their own. It's because of these compounds that certain cannabis groups leave users feeling sleepy or motivated. Depending on the concentration of certain terpenes, a cannabis strain will display a specific type of effect. For example, the limonene terpene has an incredibly pungent lemon aroma and taste; as well as the ability to reduce stress and elevate your mood.

In contrast, the terpene myrcene is known to be responsible for strong sedative effects. This compound is known as the couchlock terpene, and landrace indica strains likely contain high levels of it.

The Origins of *Cannabis sativa*

Cannabis sativa's native habitat is located in tropical and subtropical regions of the world. South Africa, Mexico, Panama, Colombia, Malawi, Vietnam, Laos, Cambodia, and Mozambique are all home to landrace sativa strains. These regions have the ideal climate that allows sativa species to thrive. High levels of humidity, long summers, and intense light are all factors that have made sativas into what they are today.

Cannabis sativa plants grow similarly to a Christmas tree. Their tall stature is necessary to compete with other plant species for the Sun's nurturing rays. Since every inch counts in the jungle or temperate forest, sativa strains have large leaves with many thin leaflets.

The flowers that crown sativa strains are typically large and spear-like. Their buds are airy because of the humid conditions. If they were as dense as indica strains, then they would likely become moldy before the buds are pollinated.

The Effects of *Cannabis sativa*

In general, it's believed that sativa strains produce a mental high. This is because sativa strains typically make users feel motivated, euphoric, and full of energy. There are even some landrace sativa strains that can produce effects that are best described as hallucinogenic. Due to the mind-altering effects of sativa varieties, these strains are usually left to those that can handle a more mental experience.

It's common for beginners to become paranoid or frightened when experiencing the effects of a sativa. Even hardened cannabis veterans can succumb to the overwhelming effects of landrace sativa strains.

On the other hand, landrace sativas can provide an overwhelmingly enjoyable experience with a boost of creativity, energy, and awareness. Not all of us want to become couch potatoes, and sativa strains are ideal for daytime use and pair easily with most outdoor activities.

What types of activities can sativa strains make more enjoyable? Let's take a look.

- Hiking
- Running
- Swimming
- Intimate activities with your partner
- Weight lifting
- Cleaning
- Shopping
- Socializing
- Meditation
- Eating
- Studying

With so many use cases, sativa strains are highly functional that can make any dull day into a bright one. As we mentioned at the beginning of this article - these effects are primarily the result of terpenes. In the case of landrace sativas, the most common terpenes found in high concentrations are limonene, pinene, caryophyllene, and humulene.

Each of these terpenes influences the aroma and flavor profile, as well as endow sativa strains with effects such as increased creativity, mood, appetite, and energy.

Popular Sativa Strains

Now that you understand the unique characteristics that relate to sativa strains let's take a look at popular sativa strains that are well worth a try.

- Super Silver Haze
- Sour Diesel
- Jack Herer
- Lemon Haze
- Panama Gold
- Colombian Gold
- Malawi Gold
- Durban Poison
- Swazi Gold
- Amnesia
- Chocolope
- Haze

Not all of the strains mentioned above are landrace sativa strains. Some are hybrids that are overwhelmingly sativa (sativa-dominant hybrids). If you're curious about the word *hybrid*, we'll discuss hybrid groups later in this article.

The Origins of *Cannabis indica*

Cannabis indica strains can be found in arid, cold, mountainous, and seasonal climates. Countries that contain landrace indica strains are Afghanistan, Pakistan, Uzbekistan, Nepal, India, Iran, Lebanon, and China. Indicas are typically found in mountain ranges or within deep valleys along a natural river. If the word kush rings a bell, then you shouldn't be surprised that that particular indica strain originated in the Hindu Kush mountain range.

Botanists believe the marijuana plants evolved within Central Asia and then radiated throughout the world as humans began using it for various purposes. Although it's up for speculation, the first cannabis plants could have been of the indica variety.

Indica plants are easy to spot because they're short in stature and grow in a bush-like manner. Rather than reaching for the stars, indica plants grow wide to cover a large swath of earth. Since their environment isn't an endless battle for the light, they can grow without competition. The leaves are broad, and the leaflets are far wider than their sativa counterparts.

If you ever place an indica bud next to a sativa flower, you'll immediately realize that indica flowers are far denser. The environment plays a crucial role, and the flowers are naturally dense to retain the moisture within. The dry, hot, and windy conditions that most of these regions exhibit would quickly dry out a sativa bud in a matter of days.

Indica plants protect their offspring by encasing the seeds in a humid environment until the seeds are fully developed. This guarantees that the next generation will have a chance. Luckily for indica plants, they flower in a short period to avoid the incoming Winter conditions.

The Effects of *Cannabis indica*

Indica strains are known to make you incredibly sleepy or numb to the world. Although most indica strain descriptions start with those two attributes - there's so much more to indica varieties than meets the eye.

Indica varieties are known to be heavily relaxing. They're the perfect option for those that need to *slow down* - especially after a long shift at work. Additionally, indica strains contain terpenes that are known to produce medicinal effects, such as decrease inflammation, pain, and anxiety.

These attributes allow indica strains to be used for a profound effect on your body. Whereas sativa strains impact your mental state, indica varieties vice grip your body in hours of relaxation.

Aside from Netflix and chill, what activities are perfectly paired with *Cannabis indica*?

- Taking a *slow* nature walk
- Sleep
- Intimate activities with your partner
- Listening to music
- Eating

- Meditation

It depends on which terpenes are in an indica strain and at what concentration, but for the most part, indicas will make you fairly lethargic. Commonly, you'll feel hazy, and you will find yourself more inclined to fall asleep rather than start another episode of Game of Thrones.

The terpenes that are found in high concentrations in indica plants are myrcene, linalool, and terpinolene. Each of these produces sedative qualities, as well as anti-inflammation, anti-pain, and anti-insomnia properties.

Popular *Cannabis indica* Strains

Indica strains are the most popular varieties of marijuana dispensaries. They may be in the spotlight due to their soothing qualities and the sheer abundance of indica strains. This is because most growers cultivate indicas because they have shorter production times than sativas. Without further ado, here's a list of popular indica strains.

- Master Kush
- Bubba Kush
- Granddaddy Purple
- Blackberry Kush
- Hindu Kush
- G13
- Hash Plant
- Herijuana
- Black Domina
- Blueberry

As you can tell, most pure indica strains contain kush. This is because kush varieties that are native to Afghanistan, Nepal, and Pakistan contain narcotic effects.

What Are Hybrids?

Now, this is where cannabis strains become tricky. When we're discussing the differences between landrace (native) indica and sativa strains - we're discussing two groups that are nearly extinct. Pure indicas and sativas rarely exist in nature due to hybridization. Just as early humans helped spread cannabis around the world, modern humans are spreading hybrid cannabis strains.

In our globalized world, marijuana cultivators have access to strains that are grown around the world. Seed breeders have crossed a plethora of strains to create new flavors, aromas, and extraordinarily high THC concentrations. Prior to hybridization, landrace strains ranged between 10-20% THC. As breeders become more sophisticated and have access to nearly any strain, marijuana flowers have tested an eye-popping 35%.

Hybridization occurs when the mother is an indica, and the father is a sativa - or vice versa. This offspring is a hybrid because it contains traits that are found in both its mother and father. Hybrids have the potential to contain a multitude of effects, aromas, and flavors. For example, the hybrid Blue Dream relaxes the body while elevating the mind.

When you're in a dispensary, you'll want to know if a hybrid is *indica-dominant* or *sativa dominant*. By gaining this knowledge, you know what to expect when you indulge in a strain that leans more towards its sativa qualities.

The Effects of Hybrids

As stated previously, hybrids contain a mixture of indica and sativa effects. It's typical for users indulging in hybrids to feel motivated during the first half of the high and then covered with a blanket of calm and sleepiness during the comedown phase.

Breeders who produce hybrids take these strains a step further by using strains with specific traits to produce a fine-tuned hybrid. It's common to find hybrids that have been produced from a parental lineage that's been tweaked over the course of years to produce a very specific effect. This could mean a hybrid with a high percentage of CBD or a strain that's perfect for chemotherapy patients.

Popular Hybrid Strains

- Blue Dream (sativa-dominant hybrid)
- Girl Scout Cookies (GSC) (indica-dominant hybrid)
- Gorilla Glue #4 (indica-dominant hybrid)
- Cherry Pie (sativa-dominant hybrid)
- Gelato (indica-dominant hybrid)
- Cheese (indica-dominant hybrid)
- White Widow (indica-dominant hybrid)

Each of these strains (and many more) exhibits a multitude of features. Sky-high mental effects and bone-crushing bodily sensations can all be felt within a single strain. If you couldn't decide between being couch-locked or in an academic state, then a hybrid is your best option to experience all of these effects at once.

Although hybrids sound like the logical next step, it also ensures the demise of landrace indica and sativa strains. These native varieties are no longer being produced because hybrids *generally* out-compete them in terms of relevance, taste, aroma, potency, and ease-of-growth.

The Power To Choose The Cannabis Strain *You* Desire

Now that you understand the inherent differences between indicas, sativas, and hybrids - you're empowered to make a decision when you're browsing a dispensary. As long as the dispensary in question tests their marijuana strains, you'll have access to a terpene report and THC or CBD concentration analysis.

Legalization has forced the cannabis industry to standardize testing, which keeps you informed on any cannabis product you choose to consume. As long as the products you use are fully tested, you'll always be able to choose a marijuana strain that fits your needs and desires.

POP QUIZ

Question #1: (BLANK) contain a mixture of indica and sativa effects.

Answer: _____

Question #2: Hybridization occurs when...

Answer: _____

Question #3: Name 5 popular indica strains.

Answer: _____

Hemp VS Marijuana...

(Shown Above: Hemp growing naturally outdoors.)

When asked, the majority of people believe that hemp and marijuana are one and the same. Although there is a sliver of truth to this, they are still incorrect. Understanding the differences between hemp and marijuana is crucial, whether you're seeking to buy a hemp-based supplement or a THC-infused product.

Join us as we delve into the vast differences between hemp and marijuana, and what each is used for.

Let's Talk About Hemp...

Hemp *is* cannabis. Its scientific classification is *Cannabis sativa ssp.*, meaning it's a subspecies of the Sativa group. After countless years of breeding, most hemp cultivars don't contain THC - the psychoactive cannabinoid that's known for getting people high.

Hemp has been used for a wide variety of applications for thousands of years, and archeologists have found hemp seeds in archeological sites on the Oki Islands (Japan) that are believed to be over 8,000-years old. There is far more evidence of hemp being used as fiber as early as 3,500BC in many Eastern Asia locations. It's believed that hemp is one of the first plants that early civilizations domesticated to produce food, fibers, and building materials.

The Uses of Hemp

Hemp is one of the most useful materials on the planet. Throughout human history, hemp has always played a crucial role in many civilizations. It wasn't until cannabis prohibition swept the globe and included hemp into the banned list. It wasn't until recently that innovators have begun using hemp again because of its many applications.

Medicine

You've probably heard of hemp due to the fact that most CBD products are derived from it. CBD is most commonly found in hemp cultivars and processed into oil. This oil is then placed into pills, balms, vaporizer cartridges, or wax.

(*Shown Above: CBD oil that is derived from Hemp.*)

Additionally, CBG is also found in large quantities within hemp varieties. CBG isn't found in significant levels of marijuana because CBG is the precursor to producing THC. Since there isn't any notable THC in hemp, the CBG is not used and thus does not disappear.

Both CBD and CBG are processed from the hemp flowers by the use of various extraction techniques. The most popular form of extracting CBD from hemp is by using a CO_2 extraction machine. This technique is far safer than solvent-based methods, such as butane - which is commonly used in extracting cannabinoids in cannabis.

Food

Have you noticed the sudden rise in hemp seeds throughout local grocery stories? We have too, and that's because hemp seeds are literally *packed* with massive amounts of vital nutrients, minerals, and protein. It just so happens that these tiny seeds are the new superfood of our generation, and it appears that it's finally here to stay.

(Shown Left: Hemp protein powder.)

Hemp seeds are a primary source of omega-3-6 fatty acids, which is beneficial for many things in your body. Omega-3-6 can reduce anxiety and depression, promote brain health, increase eye health, and reduce your risk of heart disease.

Hemp seeds are particularly popular as protein powder because they provide every amino acid to be deemed to a protein source. In every 30-grams of hemp seeds (2-3 tablespoons), there are 11-grams of available protein.

Beauty Products and Skincare

Hemp seeds are incredibly multi-purpose, as they are also used to extract hemp seed oil. Hemp seed oil is filled with hydrating and protective vitamins, such as vitamin E, A, and C. It's fro these vitamins that hemp seed oil has become a popular material for many skincare and beauty brands.

(Shown Right: CBD lotion often referred to as a "topical".)

Vitamin E has historically been used in many beauty and skincare products because it protects your skin from UV damage, fights against acne, and increases the overall health of your skin.

Vitamin A is known for stimulating cells that develop skin tissues that are responsible for firm and healthy skin.

With so many essential vitamins and minerals, hemp is likely to be found in skincare or beauty products that you use soon.

Fiber

Hemp has been used for thousands of years as a natural fiber. The stalks of hemp proved to be perfect for processing into clothes, shoes, fabrics, and other day to day necessities.

(Shown Right: Hemp string made from the fibers of the stalk.)

Construction Materials

Unsurprisingly, hemp is ideal for construction materials. What was once commonly used for creating effective insulation in the past, has found its way to the present day. Hempcrete is a form of sustainable concrete that's made primarily out of hemp and lime. Its incredible properties allow it to dissipate heat in the summer and retain warmth in the winter.

(Shown Left: Hempcrete only takes 3 ingredients to make.)

Additionally, hempcrete is known to sequester massive amounts of CO_2, which helps to mitigate global warming.

Plastic Materials

There's been a growing trend in using hemp for everyday materials, specifically plastic. Plastic has become the bane of the world due to its non-sustainable compounds, but hemp is far more biodegradable.

Other Uses

Aside from the materials previously mentioned, hemp is also used to create paper products, jewelry, and biofuel. The uses are nearly endless, and the biggest fact is that hemp is a low-impact crop. Low-impact means that it doesn't require high amounts of water or nutrients.

Ultimately, it's important that the *entire* hemp plant can be used to create something. This is why hemp is by far more sustainable than cannabis.

Unlike hemp, marijuana isn't used for building materials or raw products. Its sole use is that of recreational, spiritual, and medicinal purposes.

How Many Hemp Cultivars Exist?

Currently, there are roughly 52 approved hemp cultivars that are available to cultivators. Each has a scientific name, such as HK-08 and X-59, and this shows the significant different versus marijuana strains. Nearly all of the hemp cultivars that are used today have been created under strict controls to ensure that each plant does not produce more than 0.3% THC.

Additionally, some of the hemp cultivars that exist are best for gaining textiles, whereas others are ideal for extracting large amounts of CBD.

Hemp Cultivation

Hemp is *only* grown outdoors, and you'll never find an indoor hemp production facility. Hemp is grown closely together, similar to that of corn, and males are allowed to grow interspersed among the females. This is because hemp producers *want* their crops to be pollinated because of the value of hemp seeds.

Once the hemp seeds are mature, the entire field of hemp is cut down. Since the entire hemp plant can be used for producing something, everything is harvested. From the base of the stalk to the calyxes that hold the seeds - nothing but the roots are left behind.

The Legality of Hemp

Ever since cannabis legalization became mainstream, the focus has shifted towards CBD and hemp cultivation. In a landmark event, the United States passed the Farm Bill in 2018, which allows farmers to cultivate hemp - as long as it contained less than 0.3% THC.

Aside from the USA, many countries either allow the cultivation of hemp or are beginning to ease their restrictions. Canada, France, Germany, Russia, Egypt, Portugal, and Ukraine all produce hemp.

Compared the THC-rich cannabis, hemp enjoys a significant amount of freedom. Hemp and hemp products can cross state lines, sell online, and are widely available throughout the world.

Cannabis, on the other hand, is still roundly prohibited in a handful of US states, can't cross state lines, and is federally illegal.

Hemp and CBD

Hemp has gained its notoriety primarily because of CBD production. Although CBD occurs in THC-rich cannabis, the amounts are low. Alternatively, it was found that hemp cultivars contained far more CBD, which is a non-psychoactive cannabinoid.

The CBD craze has since taken off, and now, it can be found in local grocery stores near you. This sudden acceptance threw hemp into the spotlight and is now regarded as the primary way to produce CBD. All countries that allow CBD products to be bought and sold must come from CBD that's derived from hemp, and it must not contain more than 0.3% THC.

Hemp is the ideal vehicle for CBD, especially now that CBD is considered as a supplement. Although the FDA has yet to make a decision on the classification of hemp-derived CBD, it's commonly available in health food stores and grocery outlets.

These products come in the form of vape cartridges, creams, oils, and edibles.

Other Cannabinoids

Other cannabinoids can be found within hemp cultivars. THC exists in hemp, but in tiny amounts, hence the 0.3% THC requirement for most hemp varieties. CBN, CBG, CBC, and many more can be found within hemp, but not in high amounts. However, hemp cultivars are beginning to take a closer look at CBG (cannabigerol) due to its health benefits, and are seeking hemp cultivars that contain larger amounts of it.

Trichome Production

Unlike cannabis varieties, hemp cultivars do not exhibit the intense coverage of resin. Although trichomes exist on hemp, since that's where the phytocannabinoids reside, it does not mimic that of cannabis flowers.

(Shown Right: 80x zoom of trichomes on a hemp plant during the flowering phase.)

Smoking Hemp

Although you can technically smoke hemp flowers, you're better off using extracted products, such as CBD oil. This is a major difference from when compared with cannabis since one of the most popular ways of using marijuana is by smoking the flowers. This is due in part to people not drying and curing hemp flower properly.

Hemp is Eco-Friendly

Unlike cannabis, hemp is eco-friendly and does not pollute the world. Cannabis requires massive amounts of electricity when cultivated indoors. Many cultivators use dangerous pesticides to keep bugs and mold off of their prized crops, which taint the surrounding environment. Cannabis requires large amounts of water, and only the flowers are harvested.

Hemp, on the other hand, is incredibly green. Every portion of the plant can be used, and by-products, such as hempcrete, sequester massive amounts of CO_2 which further offsets its carbon footprint. As the world seeks to counter the disastrous effects of global warming, more are looking towards hemp to use as a primary base material.

What about Marijuana aka Cannabis?

Cannabis - the section you've probably been waiting for. The primary difference between cannabis and hemp is that cannabis is bred to contain THC - and lots of it. Cannabis contains three primary groups: *Cannabis sativa, Cannabis indica,* and *Cannabis ruderalis*. Let's take a look at each.

- ***Cannabis sativa***

  Cannabis sativa is well known for its Christmas tree-like growth, and it's the species that contain hemp. However, *Cannabis sativa* is known for its uplifting, motivating, and soaring mental highs.

- ***Cannabis indica***

  Indicas are known to be short and bushy plants. Indica varieties produce an intense full-body relaxation and are a beneficial tool in falling asleep.

- ***Cannabis ruderalis***

  Ruderalis is a small group that produces autoflowering genetics. Autoflowering means that these plants rely on an internal clock to begin flowering, instead of the change in light hours. When a Sativa or Indica reacts to the change in light, this is called *photoperiodism*. Instead of requiring a certain amount of light to induce flowering, Ruderalis has its' own internal guiding light.

Marijuana Production

Cannabis, on the other hand, is produced by selecting only females. Unless breeding new cannabis seeds, males are discarded once they're discovered. Cannabis seeds come in a variety of forms, such as feminized (only female), regular (male and female), and autoflowering (ruderalis genetics).

(Shown Below: Cannabis grown indoors typically provides a higher quality product.)

Cannabis is cultivated indoors and outdoors. For many, indoor cannabis is considered the very best, whereas outdoors is considered low-quality.

Instead of placing cannabis plants close together similarly to hemp crops, they are each given considerable distance. The reason for the large spacing with marijuana plants is to deter mold and fungi from growing. When plants are placed close together, the instance of fungi or mold is much higher, and cannabis crops are very susceptible.

Marijuana Harvest and Post-Harvest

Unlike hemp, marijuana is harvested *usually* with the utmost care. This means that it's not harvested by an automated combine, but rather, by hand.

The stalks are cut away, and each branch that holds a flower-covered in resin is removed. The flowers undergo a slight trim at first, primarily to remove the large fan leaves. Next, the branches and flowers are hung upside down in a drying room.

(Shown Right: Cannabis hung upside down in order to make the drying process a little more user friendly.)

The drying process can take anywhere from 4-12 days, depending on the size of the harvest. Once the buds are slightly dry, they are sent through their final manicuring process. Once done, the buds are snipped away from the branches and are placed into glass jars.

The final step is the curing process. Curing can take anywhere from 2-weeks to 2-months, depending on a cultivator's patience. Each day, the flowers are removed to allow the excess moisture and volatile gasses dissipate. This is a tedious process, but it's necessary to enhance the overall flavor and aroma of marijuana flowers.

Overall, the harvest process lasts anywhere from 1-month to 3-months, which goes to show the drastic difference in the harvest process compared to that of hemp.

THC Content

Marijuana flowers contain large amounts of cannabinoids, primarily THC. THC is a psychoactive cannabinoid, and it's the reason why you feel high when you smoke cannabis. Unlike hemp, cannabis typically contains an average of 16-22% THC. The highest recorded amount of THC is so far, 35%. Remember, hemp varieties only contain 0.3% THC or less.

It's also due to this high amount of THC that marijuana has found itself in the land of prohibition. The psychoactive effects of THC are the cause of cannabis' labeling as a drug, and it's for this reason that the federal government deemed it as a Schedule I substance. Although enough research clearly shows that cannabis/THC is not dangerous, the federal government has continued to keep the rhetoric that marijuana poses a threat.

Cannabis Varieties

Originally, there were a limited number of *landrace* cannabis varieties. Landrace means that the strains were indigenous to a specific region. It wasn't until cannabis cultivation exploded in the 1960s did most of these landrace varieties disappear. They disappeared because of hybridization, which is the fusion of two separate strains.

Although the result is far fewer landrace cannabis strain, it caused an avalanche of hybrid marijuana strains with a multitude of aromas, flavors, and effects. To this day, there are well over 3,000 strains. 3,000 is an incredibly conservative estimate, and this number dwarfs the number of hemp cultivars in existence. This abundance of marijuana strains clearly shows that marijuana varieties are in *high* demand. (*Visit the "Sativa vs Indica" section for more information.*)

Effects of THC

THC is capable of producing effects that can be experienced from CBD derived from hemp. A decrease in pain, reduced anxiety, a reduction in muscle spasms, and relief from insomnia are common examples that users swear by.

THC can drastically affect your motor skills, memory function, and emotions - all of which are very different from CBD and CBG that's derived from hemp. The primary effects are euphoria, extreme drowsiness, appetite increase, laughter, and confusion. (*Visit the "Predicting Strain Effects from THC and CBD levels" section for more information.*)

Marijuana Products

There are a vast number of different types of marijuana products. You can find a plethora of edibles, vape cartridges, flowers, oils, concentrates, and creams filled with THC. (*Visit the "Different Ways to Smoke and Consume Cannabis" section for more information.*)

Early Civilization Cannabis Use

Similar to hemp, cannabis has been used by ancient civilizations for thousands of years. It's been found in ancient gravesites and other important archeological digs. The oldest written record of cannabis use is from Herodotus (440BC). (*Visit the "History of Cannabis" section for more information.*)

POP QUIZ

Question #1: (BLANK) is a small group that produces autoflowering genetics.

Answer: _____

Question #2: United States passed the Farm Bill in 2018, which allows farmers to cultivate hemp - as long as it contained less than (BLANK) THC.

Answer: _____

Question #3: Alternatively, it was found that (BLANK) cultivars contained far more CBD.

Answer: _____

Types of Cannabis: The Difference Between Dank, Mids, and Reggie...

Although there are a plethora of cannabis strains, *quality* is the deciding factor if a flower is considered dank, mids, or reggie. In cannabis culture, these three slang terms adequately describe the overall quality of dried flowers, such as the trichome coverage, flavor, aroma, potency, and overall look.

Read along to understand these three grades, so you understand what's considered the best - and what's not.

Dank, Top Shelf Cannabis

Cannabis flowers that are dank are considered the best quality that money can buy. You've probably heard a handful of other terms that are one the same level as dank, such as fire, top-shelf, private reserve, head-stash, headies, and loud.

When you're at your local cannabis dispensary, and the budtender says that a certain strain is "pure fire," then it better look the part.

How can you determine the dankness of weed? Here are the traits you need to visually look at to determine if a flower is top-shelf.

(Shown Left: Top shelf cannabis. Photo Credits: East Bay Express)

Trichome Coverage

Plain and simple, if the frost is lacking, then you're about to get ripped off. Top-shelf cannabis strains are supposed to be the cream of the crop, and they *need* to be drenched in frost. This layer of resin will also give you a foreboding of the THC content that it potentially contains.

When you put your finger on the flower, it should immediately become sticky. Up close, you should be able to see intact trichome heads that are bursting with THC. Since trichomes are the outer layer of the cannabis flower, this aspect should strike you first. If you don't feel overwhelmed by the coverage, move along until something shocks you.

Aroma

The aroma should be *loud*. When marijuana enthusiasts call a strain loud, they're referring to its invasive and offensive aroma. Of course, some of us prefer to be discreet when using marijuana, but nonetheless - the loudness of a strain is a significant factor in determining the dankness of a strain.

There are so many different aromas found in marijuana, and the flower should literally *reek* of the dominating smell. If a strain is known for its lemon peel-covered-in-fuel aroma, then your nose should catch these characteristics immediately. Once a budtender opens a jar filled with the strain, the aroma should be *very* noticeable. If the aroma doesn't strike you or seems bland - then it's probably not top-shelf.

Taste

You can only taste a strain once you've bought it. Therefore, you'll need to determine if a strain is top-shelf before getting to try it. Once you've made a purchase - it's time to put it to the ultimate test.

The taste should contain many characteristics of the aroma, and it should be very noticeable. With most high-quality cannabis flowers, the smoke should coat your mouth with an incredible resin. As the effects take hold, you'll notice the flavors on your palate even more so.

Effects

Fire weed should have heavy-hitting effects. The final test for dank weed is to get knocked back by its effects. Before purchasing a strain, you should always make sure to find the THC concentration. This will give you a good idea of what to expect, but it doesn't always give the entire picture. Terpenes play a significant role in the effects of THC, and most dispensaries don't show terpene concentrations.

However, the outright potency of the strain should be mind-blowing. If the effects don't make you say, "That's the strongest weed I've ever tried," then it's probably not as top-shelf as you originally thought.

Overall Look

The buds should look impressive. The buds should be full, whether spear-shaped or golfball-shaped. The buds shouldn't look like they've been handled by 10,000 people, but instead, they should look delicate and fresh. When buying top-shelf cannabis, you need to become a connoisseur to sift through the chaff to get to the marijuana that's worth trying.

What are Mids?

Mids are the classification for middle-of-the-road cannabis flowers. This category's quality can be described as good, not bad, but not great. Other names that the cannabis community call mids by is chronic, beasters, and regs. Let's take a look at the various factors that classify cannabis flowers as mids.

(Shown Above: Mid-grade cannabis. Photo Credits: 420 Magazine)

Trichome Coverage

When it comes to the trichome coverage, mids contain a decent amount of resin. The resin coverage won't wow you, but it will look leave you feeling inclined - if the price is right. If you look at mids, the trichomes will look broken in places due to them being handled poorly during harvest, transportation, or at the dispensary.

Aroma

The aroma of mids will catch your attention, but it won't make you jump back in awe. This is because the overall scent has been reduced by poor quality management or lackluster conditions during growth, harvest, or storage.

Mids provide an adequate aroma, but they can't compete with buds that are in the private reserve category.

Taste

The taste of mids will have a significant amount of chlorophyll than compared with top-shelf cannabis. Although the aroma will find its way to the taste, it won't be so direct and robust. In other words, mids are the diluted version of top-shelf cannabis.

Effect

Since the quality of the flower is lower than that of top-shelf cannabis, the effects will suffer as well. You can still get incredibly high from mids, but it may take more to do so. When smoking mids, it may take 2-4 more extra puffs to get you where you want to be.

Overall Quality

The overall quality of mids will look like tone-down versions of top-shelf strains. The buds will be intact and look overall decent, but they won't look as fresh as dank weed.

Last and Least, Reggie Cannabis aka Brick

Reggie cannabis, also known as schwag and brick weed, is the lowest quality cannabis you can find. This category details marijuana that you should stay away from, and should only buy it if it's nearly free. Many unsuspecting buyers have bought reggie cannabis in place of what they were told was mids or even top-shelf flower.

(Shown Right: Reggie aka brick weed. Photo Credits: Vocal)

Trichome Coverage

What trichome coverage should be the question. On reggie weed, you won't find many trichomes, and if you do, they're likely broken. These flowers won't look dusted in resin, and they won't be sticky to the touch.

Aroma

The aroma of reggie weed will have an aroma, but it won't be pleasurable. It's likely that it'll smell like freshly cut grass, instead of anything else. Although fresh cut grass is a pleasant smell, it has no business being in your weed.

Flavor

The flavor, just like the aroma, will taste of grass. This won't be an enjoyable experience. The primary reason why reggie weed tastes like grass is that the grower didn't allow the chlorophyll to dissipate during the drying process. The end result is cannabis flowers that taste like hay, rather than dank cannabis.

The Process That Determines The Quality of Weed

When it comes to cannabis flowers, the overall quality of the weed will be determined during the growth, harvest, and curing process. Let's take a look at each.

Growth Process

During the growth process, cannabis plants undergo various elements, depending on whether they are grown indoors or outdoors.

(Shown Right: Grower transplanting clone. Photo Credits: Canmar Recruitment)

If a cannabis plant is grown outdoors, it's likely that it's been munched on by bug and exposed to various elements - such as wind, rain, heat, and dust. Due to this, it's unlikely that you'll find top-shelf strains grown in outdoor conditions. Although very good quality weed is grown outdoors, it's likely that it will fall into the mids category.

When grown indoors, there are far fewer elements that will affect the overall quality. The environment is in the hands of the cultivator, and they can fine-tune the setting to create perfect growing conditions. Top-shelf strains come from indoor facilities, but this takes an incredible amount of skill. Since it takes a high level of skill to grow dank weed, the majority of cannabis grown indoors is rated as meds or reggie.

Harvest Process

The harvest process is the deciding point where all those countless hours of hard work will pay off or not. The harvest process entails cutting down the canopy and beginning the drying process. This entire process will play a large role in the overall taste, effect, aroma, and look.

(Shown Left: Harvesting Cannabis. Photo Credits: Terpenes & Testing)

Once you chop the flowers down, they'll need to undergo a trim. A steady hand is necessary to trim a bud to perfection. When you pick up a flower at a dispensary, you'll be able to quickly tell if the trimmer knew what he or she was doing.

The drying process must be closely monitored, according to a certain temperature and relative humidity levels, which allow the flavors and aroma of the strain to truly blossom.

The Curing Process

This is it - the moment that any cultivator has waited months for. This process will make or break your cannabis flowers, and it's this stage that so many cultivators get wrong - which leads to vast amounts of reggie and mid weed.

(Shown Right: Curing Cannabis on Caregiver level. Photo Credits: Leafly)

The curing process allows volatile gases, such as CO_2 and trapped chlorophyll, to escape. Additionally, this process allows cannabis flowers to cure like a fine wine. The process generally takes up to 2-months and is as closely monitored as the drying process.

When done right, the aroma and flavor explode with terpenes. The potency is as high as it gets due to the perfect temperature and humidity conditions. The overall look of the flower takes on a pale hue due to the delicate processes that they've undergone.

The Cost

Now that we've explained every difference between dank, mids, and reggie weed, it's time for the last category - the price.

As most of you probably know, dank cannabis flowers demand a *high* price. We're talking at least $20 per gram or $60 per 1/8th. Of course, not all of us want to spend that amount, but when you do, it's always going to be worth it. There's nothing quite like smoking a picture-perfect cannabis bud that would look perfect in a museum display.

Mids are the most common flowers you'll find, and these come at a price of $10-15 per gram and $35-45 per 1/8th. These flowers aren't showstoppers by any means, but they will get the job done. As long as you don't pay higher than these prices - it's a deal.

Reggie weed isn't recommended unless you're getting the flowers for free, or at such a low cost that it would be a shame to pass up. These flowers look battered, but they will still get you high *at some point*. Per gram, reggie weed will cost $5 per gram or $99 per ounce. Reggie weed is only bought during moments of economic difficulties, and are never showed off.

Quality Or Quantity?

The choice is yours. If you choose quality over quantity, then you'll have less weed - but incredible weed at that. If you choose quantity over quality, then you'll have a lot of lower quality cannabis at a low price. Everything depends on you - and your determination for quality or quantity.

What is the Endocannabinoid System and What is its Function Within the Human Body?...

Whilst some individuals take cannabis to enjoy a high, increasing amounts of people are trying cannabis (and CBD in particular) for its therapeutic and medicinal benefits.

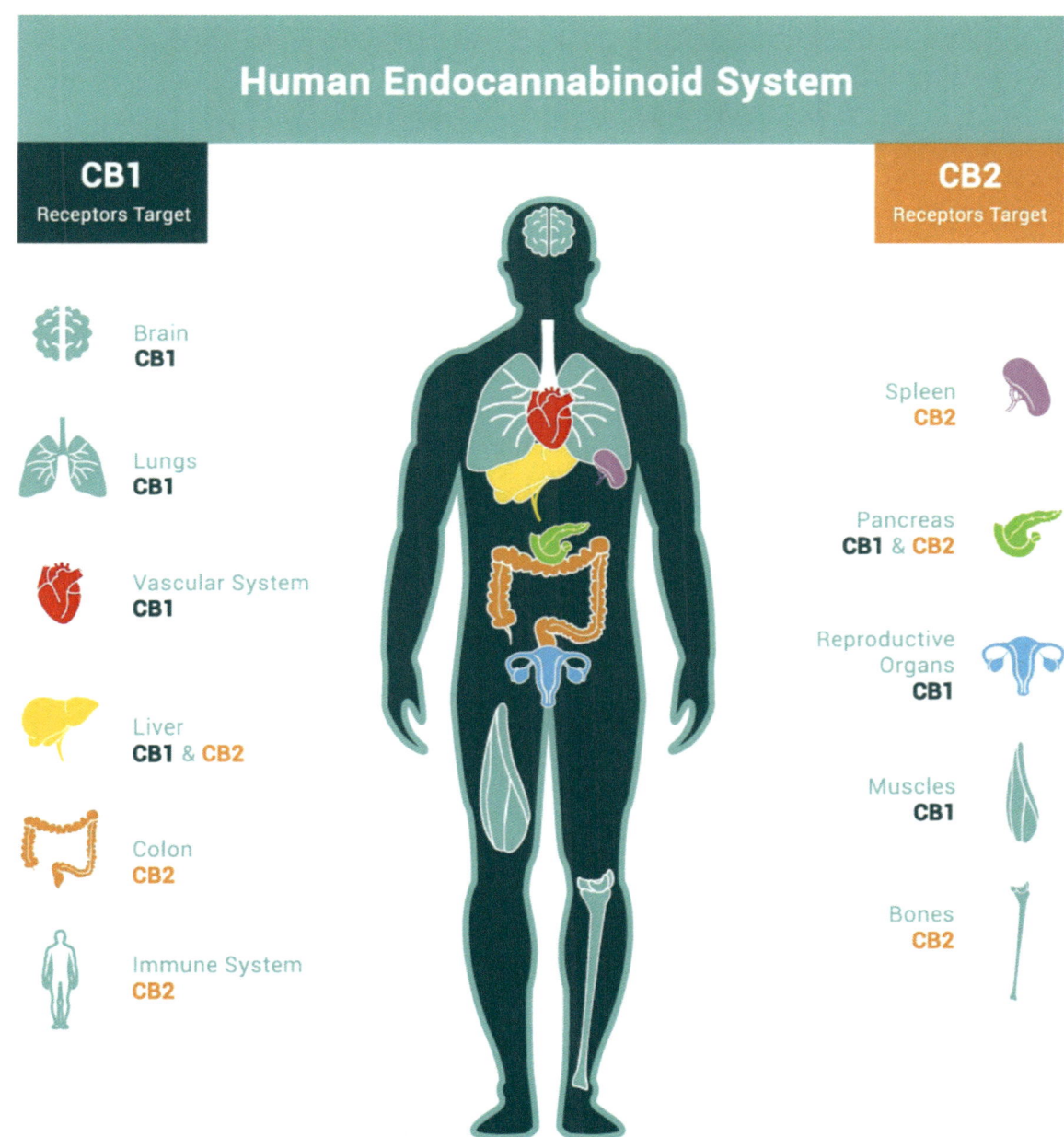

(Shown Above: Endocannabinoid System. Photo Credits: Clearleaf Labs)

What you may not know is that those feelings of euphoria (or in the case of CBD, welcome relief from troublesome symptoms) are only made possible by one of our body's most important biological regulatory structures.

This structure is known as the endocannabinoid system. This system contains an array of receptors that are capable of interacting with chemical compounds such as THC and CBD.

However, it's function isn't just to help us enjoy the beneficial effects of different cannabis-derived chemical compounds.

It serves a much higher purpose; homeostasis.

Homeostasis: Maintaining the Body's Equilibrium

Before delving into the inner-workings of the endocannabinoid system, it's useful to explain in a little more depth the importance of homeostasis in the context of our daily biological routine.

Described by many as the "Goldilocks Zone", homeostasis is the biological process of maintaining just the right conditions for our cells to perform at optimum levels.

A good way to visualize homeostasis is by thinking of your body as a set of old fashioned weighing scales. With an equal amount of ongoing biological processes on each side.

To perform cellular-level processes optimally, your body must have the scales level or at equilibrium, with one side weighing exactly the same as the other.

If one set of biological processes takes up more of the body's operating power (becoming heavier on our hypothetical scales), then our delicate cells begin to lose their ability to operate at their maximum potential.

Our body has a very narrow optimum range, and therefore homeostasis is an everlasting biological balancing act. Our endocannabinoid system is vital in our body's fight to maintain balance.

It manages to achieve this outcome by sending chemical messages in reaction to stimuli.

For example, when we are too hot, our body releases sweat to help us cool back down. Or when our blood sugar is high, insulin is released to bring those levels back to normal. All of these reactions are part of the body's goal of achieving homeostasis.

What Are the Key Components of the Endocannabinoid System (ECS)?

Due to the it's pivotal role in homeostasis, the ECS evolved millions of years ago and is present today not just in humans, but in all vertebrate species.

There are three principal components that make up the overall system which are as follows:

- **Cannabinoid Receptors** – These are located on the surface of our cells
- **Endocannabinoids** – These are the small molecules that activate the cannabinoid receptors
- **Metabolic enzymes** – These enzymes are used to break down the endocannabinoids after they've performed their function.

Firstly, let's begin with the role of the cannabinoid receptors within the ECS.

Cannabinoid Receptors

Cannabinoid receptors are best described as "listening devices" attached atop of our cells.

They are constantly monitoring conditions outside of the cell and transmitting that information back through to the cell, kick-starting appropriate cellular responses to specific stimuli.

There are multiple different cannabinoid receptors, but the most studied and understood receptors are known as CB1 and CB2.

- **CB1**

    These receptors are found in the brain and nervous system.

    They were discovered by researchers looking at the psychoactive effects of THC, and it's these receptors that react with THC to give users a "high" sensation.

    Although their presence in humans was not confirmed until the late 80s and early 90s, their importance has since been uncovered.

    They make up over 50% of the brains cannabinoid receptors, and they outnumber all other cannabinoid receptors *combined*.

When activated, CB1 receptors reduce the activity of key processes happening within a cell. They do so by flooding neurons (which send messages around the brain and nervous system) with calcium ions, preventing them from firing.

Activating CB1 receptors can have many different effects and biological reactions depending upon where the specific cell is located.

- **CB2**

    CB2 receptors are primarily found outside of the central nervous system, primarily in the immune system. They have been found to be only 44% identical to CB1 receptors, yet they still perform the same overall cellular purpose.

    The main discrepancies are the different type of cells they're located within and differences in the chemicals required to activate them.

    Since CB2 receptors are mainly found in the immune system, this means their activation reduces the activity of cells within this structure, specifically B cells.

    B cells are responsible for recognizing chemical markers of injury or illness. Once recognized, they activate T cells ("soldier" or "doctor" cells) to either fight or treat the infected area.

    To activate T cells, B cells release chemical messengers known as chemokines. When activated, CB2 receptors inhibit their ability to produce them, and raises the threshold required for T cells to be released.

Endocannabinoids

Put simply, endocannabinoids are the molecules that bind to and subsequently activate cannabinoid receptors such as CB1 and CB2.

These molecules are produced and released by the body, rather than introduced, as is the case with CBD or THC.

Unusually for biological molecules, they're synthesized on demand, which means they are created and used exactly when they are needed, rather than stored for later use.

One again, there are two main players; anandamide and 2-AG.

Anandamide

Anandamide was the first endocannabinoid to be discovered. This molecule is a partial activator (agonist) for both CB1 and CB2 receptors.

(Shown Right: Anandamide. Photo Credits: Wikipedia)

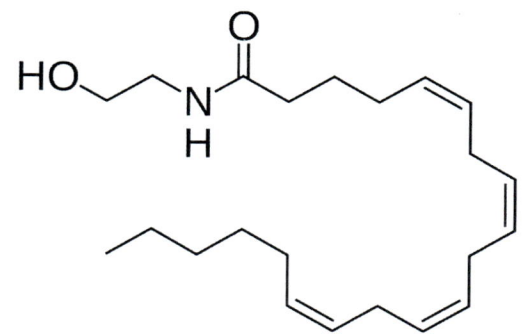

However, it is a much better agonist of CB1 than it is of CB2.

However, even when successfully bound, anandamide's activation rates max out at roughly 40% of 2-AG's comparative activation rates.

2-AG

2-AG is another important endocannabinoid that was discovered not long after anandamide.

(Shown Left: 2-AG. Photo Credits: Wikimedia)

As highlighted, 2-AG is much more potent when it comes to activating cannabinoid receptors. In fact, 2-AG is a full agonist of both CB1 and CB2 receptors.

It has also been strongly linked to the "runners high" feeling experienced by many endurance athletes after extreme physical exertion.

Metabolic Enzymes

This third component of the ECS is made up of the enzymes that break down the endocannabinoids once they've been used.

The two main enzymes utilized are FAAH and MAGL. FAAH concerns itself with breaking down anandamide, whilst MAGL focuses on taking apart 2-AG.

The main function of the enzymes is to ensure that endocannabinoids are activated and then destroyed before they have been used for too long.

It's this exact process that distinguishes endocannabinoids from the majority of molecular signals used within the body. For example, hormonal chemical messengers can be utilized for much longer and are stored for later use after completion.

How Do the Components of the ECS Work Together?

The three major components of the ECS described above are found in nearly every major structure and system within the human body.

When certain stimuli knock the body outside of its natural equilibrium (one of the sides becoming heavier or lighter in our weight scales analogy), these three elements are all called into action to redress the balance (homeostasis).

What's interesting is that the ECS is only called upon in a space- and time-selective manner, to restore the previous physiological state of homeostasis.

With this is mind, let's look a little closer at what happens in specific areas of the body when the ECS is activated, namely the firing of brain cells in the nervous system and the inflammatory response of the immune system.

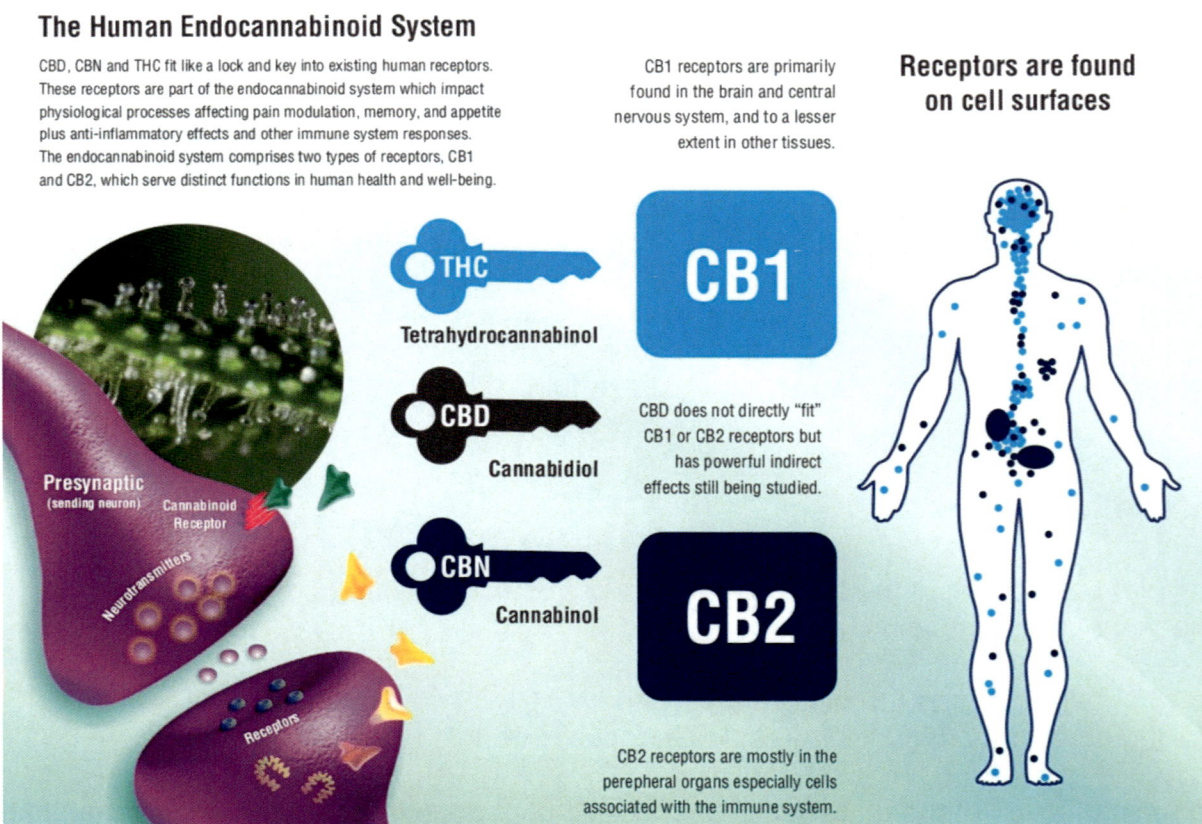

(Shown: Endocannabinoid Receptors & More. Photo Credits: Medium)

ECS Regulation of Brain Cell Firing

The neurons within our brain cells communicate with each other by sending electrochemical signals to each other. They are constantly "listening" to interconnected neurons to ascertain whether to fire its own signal or not.

However, just like with almost all systems in the body, there is a balance to be had with signals between neurons. Too many signals can overload the neuron and can prove toxic.

That is, until the ECS kicks in.

As an arbitrary example, let's say one "receiving" neuron is listening to two other "sending" neurons.

One of the "sending" neurons is firing at a normal rate, but the other is overactive and sending far too many signals. The listening neuron, recognizing this is the case, will generate and release endocannabinoids to combat the over-activity.

Once the endocannabinoids have made it to the "noisy" neuron, they bind to the CB1 receptors. As already explained, once the CB1 receptor is activated it then releases calcium ions to reduce the firing to normal levels, returning it to homeostasis.

Fascinatingly, endocannabinoids do something that neuron signals can't.

They travel backwards.

In our neural networks, signals are only sent one way from a "sending" neuron to a "receiving" neuron that listens and then acts on those signals.

However, endocannabinoids give neurons the option to regulate the amount of signals they receive by sending them back up the chain to overactive "sender" neurons. This is why endocannabinoids are known as "retrograde signals".

Whilst it's crucial to regulate biological processes in the brain, every one of our systems needs careful regulation to maintain overall homeostasis. Whether that's the endocrine or the renal system, they all require the ECS to jump in from time to time to maintain the balance.

The ECS is also activated in the immune system when injury or illness strikes. Hence, let's review the role of the ECS in the inflammation process during an immune response.

ECS Regulation of Inflammation

Inflammation is part of the immune system's response to infection or physical injury.

During this process, pathogens (germs) and damaged tissue are removed. When the body inflames an infected area, it allows the immune cells to move in to remove what's necessary to allow the body to return to its previous harmonious state.

However, problems arise when the process of inflammation lasts longer than required or spreads from the initial site requiring a response.

Chronic inflammation and auto-immune disease are both classic examples of when the immune system get activated improperly, leading to persistent inflammation or healthy cells coming under attack from our own immune system.

There has been some initial research to suggest that by tweaking the ECS, the effects of inflammatory diseases can be lessened or eradicated completely, since endocannabinoids are so instrumental in the regulation of immune responses.

This makes sense when you consider the role of the ECS during the process of an immune response triggered by a bacterial infection.

To begin with, immune cells detect the presence of the infection and send out proinflammatory signals, alerting more immune cells to come and help deal with the infection.

Whilst endocannabinoids are also generated to signal for more immune cells to respond, crucially, they *also* regulate that response so that it isn't excessive.

The pivotal ECS regulation of the immune system, allows the usual immune response to take place, whilst ensuring that it comes to a stop once the necessary restorative work has been completed.

This prevents excessive inflammation, and allows the cells within the infected area to return to a state of homeostasis.

How Do Plant-Derived Cannabinoids Interact with The ECS?

The reason that cannabis-derived cannabinoids (known as phytocannabinoids) such as THC or CBD have psychoactive or healing effects on the body is because of their interaction with the ECS.

For instance, THC gives you a "high" because it activates the CB1 receptor within the brain, much like the endocannabinoid anandamide does.

But if anandamide activates CB1 receptors in the brain naturally, then why aren't constantly in a state of euphoria?

First and foremost, it's because THC doesn't interact with the receptors in the same fashion as anandamide. Moreover, the metabolic enzymes that break down our endocannabinoids don't work on THC, so it stays in our system for a much longer period of time.

You should also note that molecules like cannabinoids rarely interact with just one or two receptor types.

Take CBD for example, it doesn't just influence cannabinoid receptors in the brain, it interacts with opioid and dopamine receptors too.

But it doesn't stop there.
CBD can have an effect on the number of endocannabinoids present in the brain (known as "endocannabinoid tone").

Since CBD inhibits the FAAH enzyme, anandamide levels increase, because there's no enzyme available to break it down.

This biological phenomenon has been used to explain the success stories of patients using CBD to treat anxiety disorders. Although clinical trials are still ongoing, it's thought that CBD's ability to increase the endocannabinoid tone of the brain is behind those early successes.

Therefore, whilst phytocannabinoids do activate CB1 and CB2 receptors, it's important to remember that they also influence the behavior of many other receptors and have an impact on overall endocannabinoid levels, creating more distinct effects on the body.

Recap – The Endocannabinoid System (ECS)

The ECS is made up of three core components, cannabinoid receptors, endocannabinoid molecules, and their metabolic enzymes.

It plays a crucial role in regulating our body's systems and maintaining the physiological equilibrium known as homeostasis.

Since the ECS plays such a pivotal role in maintaining balance within our bodies, it is used sparingly, only called into action in specific areas experiencing specific circumstances. Once homeostasis is restored, the ECS lays dormant, waiting for its next task.

Whilst it's true that the ECS can be activated by consuming phytocannabinoids such as CBD, that does not mean that everything within the body will suddenly become perfectly balanced.

Just like any other complex biological system, things can go wrong with the ECS.

If the body endures a state of prolonged absence from homeostasis, it can lose its ability to regulate its own space- and time-selective mandate, and begins interfering with cells that do not require its attention.

When this happens, unfortunately, the ECS begins to aid diseases rather than help to fight them off.

So before you start taking CBD, you must know ahead of time that it's not a cure-all drug. Our biological make-up is incredibly complex, and thus CBD products interact with everyone differently.

By gaining a deeper understanding of the ECS (and its role in maintaining homeostasis on a cellular level), you can be more appreciative of its efforts, and understand how cannabis-derived therapies help to improve its overall function.

The presence and importance of the ECS in so many of our critical biological systems such as the nervous and immune systems, helps to explain why such a wide variety of ailments have positive responses to cannabis-based treatments.

References

Roger G Pertwee. "Cannabinoid pharmacology: the first 66 years" *British Journal of Pharmacology* (2006) 147, S163–S171.
https://www.ncbi.nlm.nih.gov/pmc/articles/PMC1760722/

Herkenham M, Lynn AB, Little MD, Johnson MR, Melvin LS, De Costa BR, Rice KC. "Cannabinoid receptor localization in brain" *Proc Natl Acad Sci USA* (1990) 87, 1932–1936
https://www.ncbi.nlm.nih.gov/pubmed/2308954

Latek D, Kolinski M, Ghoshdastider U, Debinski A, Bombolewski R, Plazinska A, Jozwiak K, Filipek S. "Modeling of ligand binding to G protein coupled receptors: cannabinoid CB1, CB2 and adrenergic β 2 AR" *Journal of Molecular Modeling* (2011) 17, 9, 2353–66
https://www.ncbi.nlm.nih.gov/pubmed/21365223

Won Chang, Micah J. Niphakis, Kenneth M. Lum, Armand B. Cognetta, Chu Wang, Megan L. Matthews, Sherry Niessen, Matthew W. Buczynski, Loren H. Parsons, and Benjamin F. Cravatt. "Highly Selective Inhibitors of Monoacylglycerol Lipase Bearing a Reactive Group that Is Bioisosteric with Endocannabinoid SubstratesJae" *Chemistry & Biology* (2012) 19, 5, 579-588
https://reader.elsevier.com/reader/sd/pii/S1074552112001081?token=53E62E6FE8D77 77049ACD1B13D7A281C6E714493CDBF7D4D376D466A9A27B9312A5ACB9335CC9 9C23B633EC5260EA4D5

Ligresti A, De Petrocellis L, Di Marzo V. "From Phytocannabinoids to Cannabinoid Receptors and Endocannabinoids: Pleiotropic Physiological and Pathological Roles Through Complex Pharmacology" *Physiological Reviews* (2016) 96, 4, 1593-1659
https://www.ncbi.nlm.nih.gov/pubmed/27630175

Nagarkatti P, Pandey R, Rieder SA, Hegde VL, Nagarkatti M. "Cannabinoids as novel anti-inflammatory drugs" *Future Medinical Chemistry* (2009) 1, 7, 1333-1349
https://www.ncbi.nlm.nih.gov/pmc/articles/PMC2828614/pdf/nihms155268.pdf

POP QUIZ

Question #1: (BLANK) was the first endocannabinoid to be discovered. This molecule is a partial activator (agonist) for both CB1 and CB2 receptors.

Answer: _____

Question #2: These are the small molecules that activate the cannabinoid receptors...

Answer: _____

Question #3: When it comes to cannabis flowers, the overall quality of the weed will be determined during the growth, harvest, and (BLANK) process.

Answer: _____

What Are Cannabis Terpenes and What Do They Do?

When you unseal a jar filled with cannabis or open a pack of marijuana extract, a plethora of aromas fills the air. Just a sommelier with wine, cannabis enthusiasts are beginning to discern the wide variety of scents that are found within cannabis products.

Not only do cannabis strains play host to this multitude of scents, but it also contains seemingly endless flavor profiles. Join us as we dive into the world of terpenes to discover how they affect the flavor and aroma of cannabis.

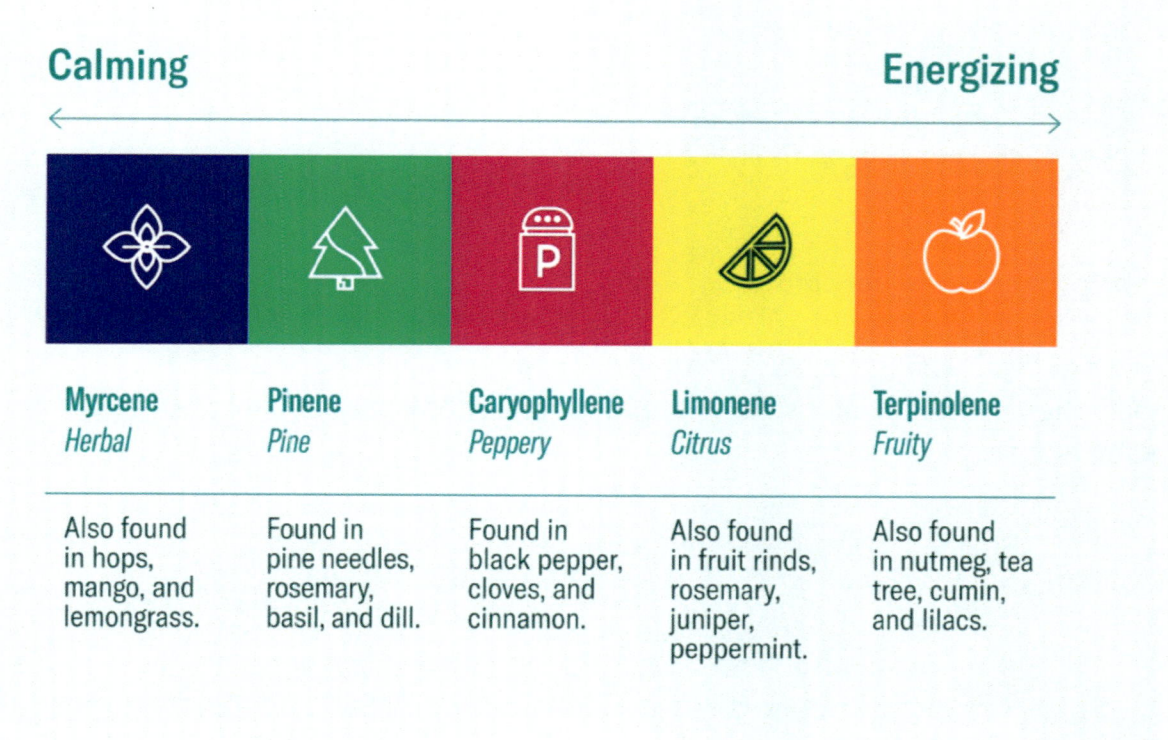

Myrcene	Pinene	Caryophyllene	Limonene	Terpinolene
Herbal	*Pine*	*Peppery*	*Citrus*	*Fruity*
Also found in hops, mango, and lemongrass.	Found in pine needles, rosemary, basil, and dill.	Found in black pepper, cloves, and cinnamon.	Also found in fruit rinds, rosemary, juniper, peppermint.	Also found in nutmeg, tea tree, cumin, and lilacs.

(Shown Above: Terpene Chart. Photo Credits: Leafly)

What Are Terpenes?

Terpenes are organic compounds that are found in nearly all plant species. These compounds are responsible for the perceived flavor and aroma in plants, and there are over 100 found in cannabis. Plants evolved the ability of terpenes for a variety of reasons; namely to deter predators and attract beneficial organisms.

Luckily for us, cannabis exhibits a wide range of enjoyable terpenes that are a pleasure to smell and taste. Additionally, terpenes interact with the endocannabinoid system, which means that it can influence the way we feel.

Do Terpenes Affect Us More Than THC and CBD?

This is the question that everyone wants to know. So far, it's known that THC is incredibly capable of psychoactive effects. Cannabidiol, also known as CBD, is primarily used to treat physical and mental issues throughout the world. Terpenes, on the other hand, are being studied in regards to how they interact with cannabinoids and the endocannabinoid system.

It appears that terpenes are capable of pushing cannabinoids to work harder, as well as display health benefits on their own.

Health Benefits of Terpenes

The most interesting discovery in relation to terpenes has been the sheer amount of health benefits associated with them. Let's take a look at a handful of terpenes and the benefits that are attributed to them.

Linalool

 Linalool is the primary terpene found in lavender, and it's responsible for decreasing depression, reducing stress, and elevating your mood. Additionally, linalool has been studied to be a neuroprotective due to its antioxidant properties.

Pinene

If you've ever walked into a pine forest, then you've smelled endless amounts of pinene. This incredibly refreshing terpene is responsible for uplifting your mood, increasing your awareness, decreasing asthmatic symptoms, decreasing inflammation, and relieving anxiety.

Caryophyllene

Caryophyllene is directly responsible for all of those spicy aromas and flavors that you can't get enough of. When you take a deep breath of black pepper, cinnamon, and cloves; you're experiencing caryophyllene.

The health benefits that are attributed to this terpene are reducing pain, anxiety, and stress. You'll immediately know you're holding a cannabis strain with copious amounts of caryophyllene when you the spicy and woody aroma exudes from the bud.

Myrcene

Myrcene is found primarily in everyone's favorite fruit: mangos. However, myrcene has been making a big splash ever since researchers found out that it's responsible for the couch-lock effect found in many Indica strains. Before this discovery, most attributed the sedated effect with a strains background, such as if it's an Indica, Sativa, or Hybrid. However, myrcene is now the focus of such effects and goes to show it's incredible power to relax your body and mind.

Linalool

Linalool is found in lavender and is responsible for the calming and therapeutic effects of cannabis. Linalool is believed to be the perfect terpene when you need to reduce stress, anxiety, inflammation, and a boost in your mood.

Limonene

There are some terpenes that occur in higher concentrations than most, and limonene is one of them. Limonene is found in citrus rinds and is most closely associated with the fresh scent of lemons. This terpene is responsible for the fruity and citrus-like aroma and flavor found in many Sativa and Sativa-dominant strains.

Limonene has been studied to elevate your mood, reduce stress, dissipate anxiety, and reduce inflammation that causes pain.

A Wide Variety of Scents and Flavors

When it comes to the flavor and scent of marijuana, you'll be shocked by the sheer number of entirely different profiles. You can find strains that smell of fresh wood, tree resin, and a profound layer of fuel. Don't be surprised when you run into a cannabis strain that's filled with blue cheese, sweet cherries, and a subtle dash of apple. The possibilities are endless when it comes to terpenes and cannabis.

Seeking High-Terpene Cannabis Strains

To enjoy the incredible benefits terpenes, you must seek them out. To know the exact terpene content of a cannabis product, it'll have to be lab tested. Lab analysis will show the content of each terpene, and by having this information, you can fine-tune your experience.

If you're seeking a cannabis strain that will put you to bed, then it's a good idea to find something with large quantities of myrcene. Looking to stay focused? Find a strain loaded with pinene. Now that you understand what terpenes are capable of, you can elevate your experience with any cannabis product to fit your every need.

The Cannabis Entourage Effect...

Marijuana contains over 100+ different molecules called cannabinoids. The plant also produces many non-cannabinoid compounds that also work with cannabinoids. All cannabis compounds work together in a unique connection known as the "Entourage effect" by different researchers, scientists and health professionals.

The Entourage effect examines the entire plant and how it can therapeutically respond to the body on many levels. An example of the entourage effect can be found when an approval of the use of synthetic THC to mitigate the side effects of chemotherapy was given by the FDA. Synthetic THC, known as marinol, has proven to be a very poor substitute for herbal therapy. Many patients reported no benefit from marinol, but when they received full treatment their symptoms were lower.

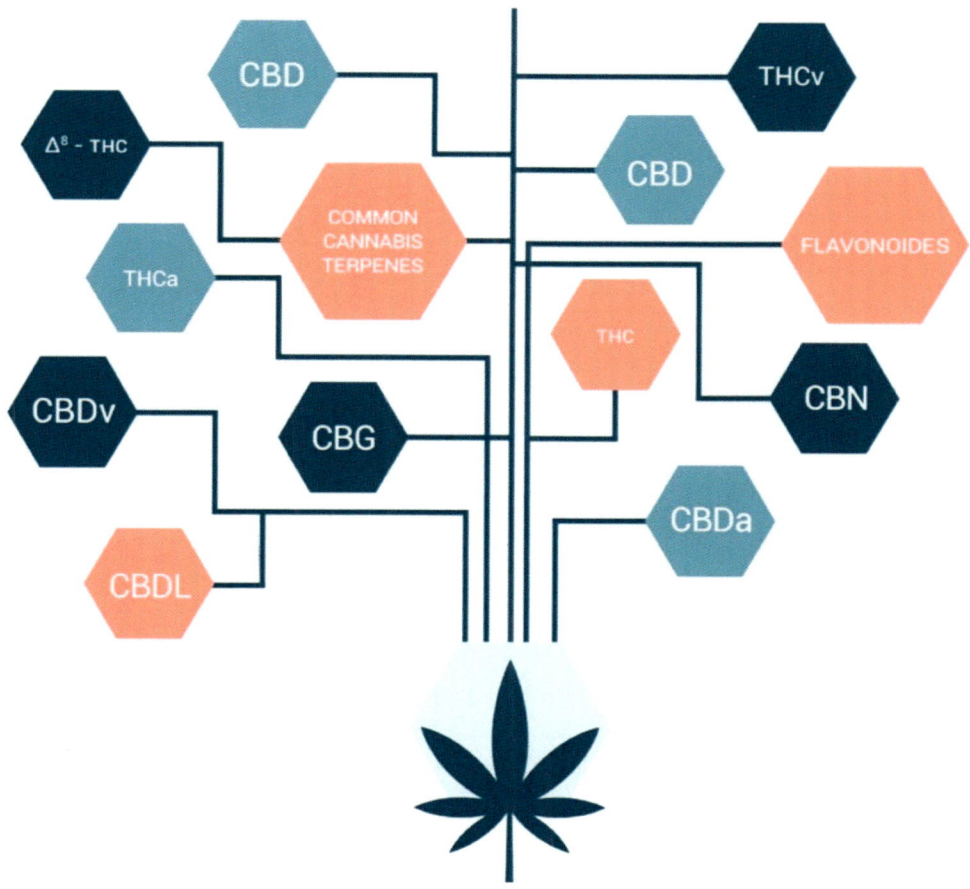

(Shown Above: Entourage Effect. Photo Credits: Cannigma)

What is the Entourage effect?

Verily it is known that cannabis buds are covered with a thick layer of crystalline resin containing hundreds of therapeutic compounds called cannabinoids and terpenoids. However, these are just two of the many important players working together to achieve certain effects. This interactive synergy between cannabis compounds and terpenoids is called the "Entourage effect", in this case this means that drugs that contain only THC or CBD are not always sufficient for many diseases.

The entourage effect is what happens when various cannabis compounds such as terpenes, THC or CBD connect together to produce a stronger effect than they have produced.

The effect of cannabis extracts may be two to four times higher than that of THC alone. This might even explain why different cannabis strains affect us in different ways. Each strain may have a slightly different terpene profile, which, in combination with known cannabis compounds, results in a different effect.

What Are THC- and CBD-Only Medicines?

Drugs containing only THC are mainly related to THC synthesis. The two best known are marinol (dronabinol) and cesamet (nabilone). These are approved medicines that are prescribed primarily for the treatment of cancer-related nausea. Their effectiveness is controversial. A 2011 study of the forms of application found that only 1.8% of the 953 patients preferred synthetic THC-based drugs to inhaled or infused methods. In addition, a pill that contains only THC can take hours to provide relief, while inhalative methods take effect immediately.

Drugs containing only CBD have gained momentum in recent years due to the media hype surrounding Charlotte's Web, a non-intoxicating cannabis strain that has been converted into a CBD-rich oil for the cure of an epileptic patient. The miraculous healing has led several states to pass laws that only apply to CBD and that THC-rich drugs are still illegal. While cannabis-based medicines containing only CBD have changed many people's lives, these laws mainly exist to help people with seizures.

Meaning of terpenes? (Brief Recap)

A terpene is an aromatic organic hydrocarbon found mainly in plants but also in some animals. Its function is to deter or attract potential pollinators. Terpenes have been honored in recent years with the legalization and growth of the marijuana industry. *(Visit the "What Are Cannabis Terpenes" section for more information.)*

What do terpenes do?

Not only are they responsible for the taste and smell of cannabis, but terpenes are also very interesting because of their healing properties. Some are known to make you more relaxed (linalol, myrcene, terpinolene), others to keep you awake (pinene, eucalyptol), while others are known for their anti-inflammatory effects (limonene, humulene, caryophyllene).

The terpenic entourage effect is very strong. For example, alpha pine, a scent of terpene-soaking pine, works well with THC and reduces the weed-degrading effect of memory. Like Dr. Russo explained that alpha-pinene can retain acetylcholine, a molecule used for memory formation, thus preventing short-term deficits. He also points out that the synergy between cannabinoids (THC and CBD) and terpenes may be useful in the treatment of depression, anxiety, cancer, inflammation, pain and bacterial infections.

As a result, today you can tell very clearly which entourage effect you want to experience. They might be able to give you the exact purpose you desire, be it a pure enjoyment you were looking for or a recovery from illness.

Can Cannabinoids and Terpenes Work Together?

The variety of chemicals that are available in whole herbal medicines is in itself remarkable, but research on how cannabinoids and terpenoids work together has been a buzz for a while now.

Ethan Russo, a neurologist who has been working on cannabis compounds and their role in the body for a long time, plays a key role in this scientific field, he explains in detail how cannabis compounds interact with each other. We're not just talking about the famous THC and CBD, even small amounts of terpenes (scented oils that smell like cannabis) can make a difference.

For example, terpenes can reduce the resistance in the blood-brain barrier, thereby facilitating the passage of other useful chemicals. Pinene helps prevent cognitive and memory disorders caused by THC. A combination of pinene, myrcene and caryophyllene terpenes helps relieve anxiety. The mixture of terpene linalool and limonene with CBD cannabinoid is promising in the treatment of MRSA. THC plus CBD produces enhanced sedative effects.

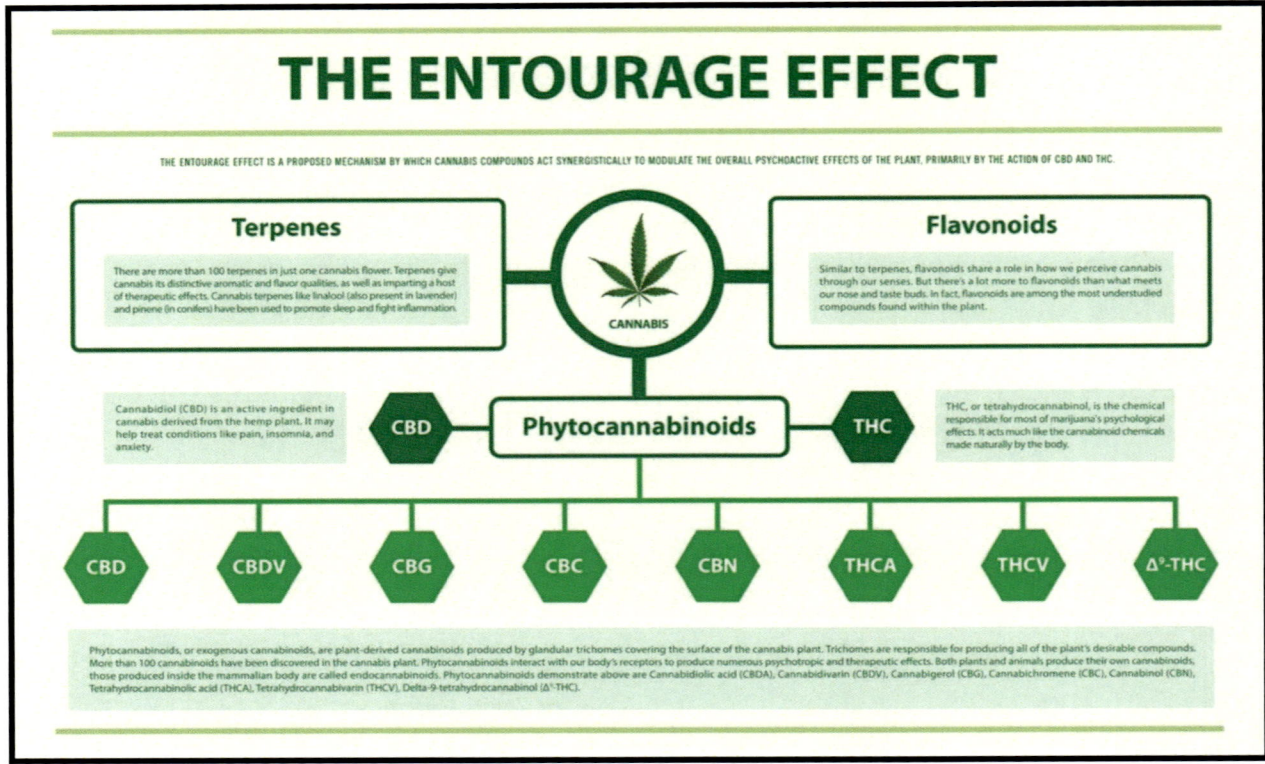

(Shown Above: Entourage Effect.)

Does Cannabis Entourage effect have side effects?

The surrounding effects of phytocannabinoids (THC and CBD) and combined terpenes and the rest of the cannabis compounds have been praised for their wonderful impact on our health. However, since there is no universal combination that is equally beneficial for any organism or at least for a particular disease, there is the possibility of a toxic effect of CBD or other compounds being presented.

For example, the ratio of CBD to THC can greatly vary from elongation to elongation. In addition, even the same strains have different connections, so you can achieve the opposite of the desired effect. Therefore, the full-spectrum surround effect is not for everyone. There is no denying that the elements of cannabis work well in unison, but for example, not everyone responds so well to full spectrum CBD oil.

In short, when we consume full cannabis (regardless of the type used, whether for consumption, smoking, topical creams, etc.), many chemical reactions occur in our body that have a powerful effect of developing environment, phytocannabinoids and terpenes, that bind to ours. Because of this, it is difficult to accurately predict how we will react and whether our condition will improve significantly or that it will lead to chaos.

Note: More research is ongoing on the Cannabis Entourage effect. However, the more we learn about the interactions between cannabinoids and terpenes, the greater the potential for full utilization of the cannabis plant.

Reference

https://www.ncbi.nlm.nih.gov/pmc/articles/PMC6334252/

https://www.scientificamerican.com/article/some-of-the-parts-is-marijuana-rsquo-s-ldquo-entourage-effect-rdquo-scientifically-valid/

https://mjbizdaily.com/entourage-effect-marketing-by-cannabis-companies/

POP QUIZ

Question #1: For example, (BLANK), a scent of terpene-soaking pine, works well with THC and reduces the weed-degrading effect of memory.

Answer: _____

Question #2: (BLANK) is now the focus of such effects and goes to show it's incredible power to relax your body and mind.

Answer: _____

Question #3: Cannabis contains over how many different molecules called cannabinoids?

Answer: _____

Predicting Strain Effects From THC and CBD Levels...

Now that cannabis is widely available throughout many states, consumers are seeking guidance on how to choose strains for particular effects. The two most prominent cannabinoids, THC and CBD, have unique differences that leverage varying effects. Read along to learn how you can predict a strains' effects by looking at its THC and CBD levels.

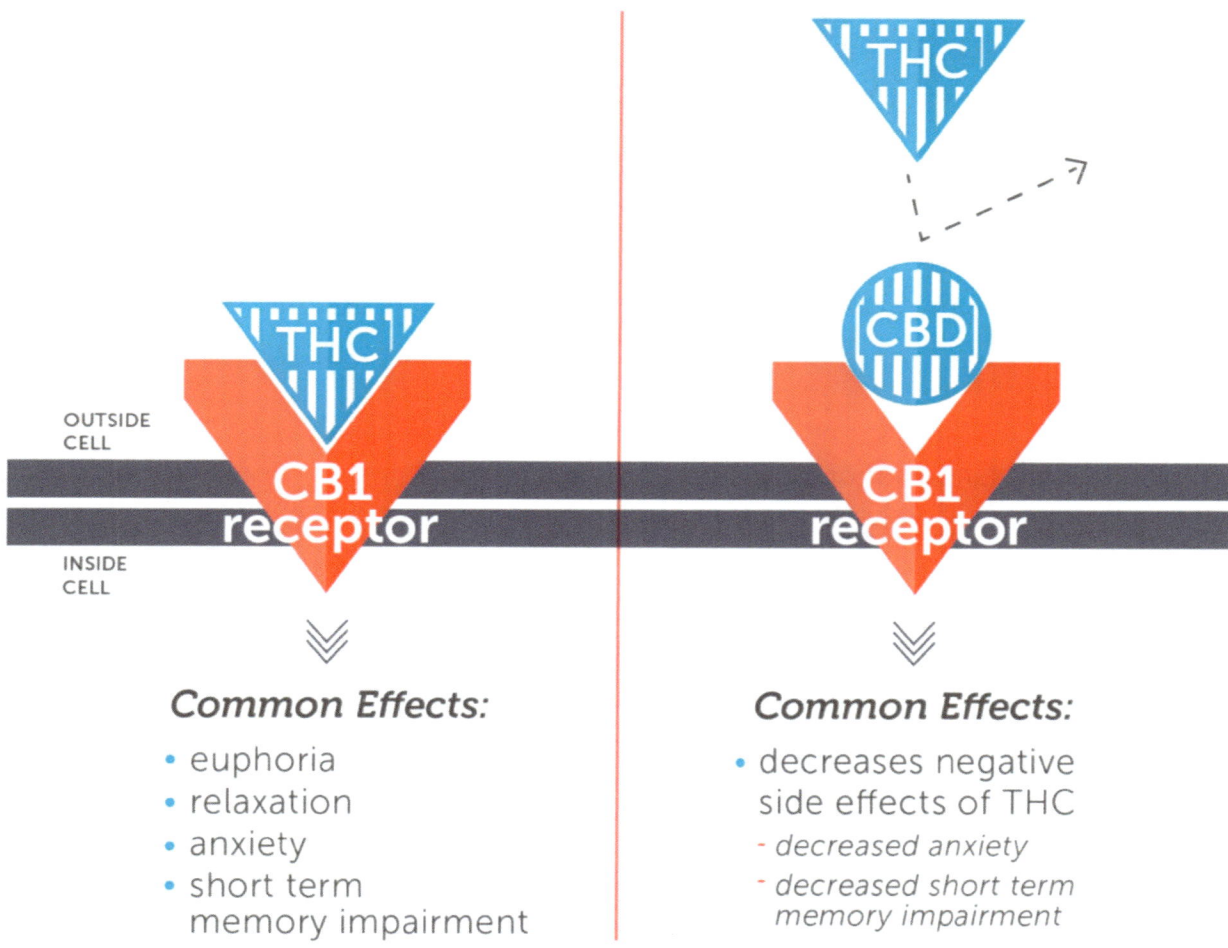

(Shown Above: THC vs CBD. Photo Credits: Leafly)

Fine-Tune Your Cannabis Experience

Although many individuals indulge in cannabis for its recreational use, there's a growing number of people who're searching for something *deeper*. Cannabis is capable of exhibiting effects that can make a profound difference in a person's life. There are a host of scientific studies that show cannabinoids and terpenes play a significant role in physical and mental health.

If you're a person who is seeking a specific experience, then this is the article you *need* to read. When you walk into a cannabis dispensary, the budtender will likely try and sell you on just about everything. In their words, everything is fire. Everything is loud.

What happens when you go home to indulge? You may feel disappointed as the effects appear to be lackluster, and the description has nothing to do with what you experienced. This is a common occurrence for thousands, or potentially, millions of marijuana users.

Instead, by understanding how THC, CBD, and terpenes work; you'll be adequately prepared to fine-tune your cannabis experience.

How THC Works In Your Body

Tetrahydrocannabinol, or THC, is the primary cannabinoid that's found in cannabis strains. This compound is incredibly psychoactive, and it's known for its ability to get users stoned or high. Aside from these recreational effects, THC is profoundly capable of producing medicinal effects.

The medicinal effects that THC produces come in the form of anti-anxiety, anti-nausea, pain relief, anti-spasm, and anti-depression. It can even stimulate your appetite or depending on the terpenes involved, suppress your appetite. As you begin to understand the vast capabilities of THC, you'll be surprised by the many experiences that you can have.

The primary reason why we feel the effects of THC is because of the existence of the endocannabinoid system. As you already know, the endocannabinoid system is a network of naturally occurring cannabinoids within the human body. This system contains two major receptor networks: CB1 and CB2.

THC is known to directly affect the CB1 receptor group by physically blocking it. Once this blockage occurs, neuro signals are unable to transmit, which results in your body feeling stoned or high. The CB1 receptor group is found primarily in the brain and spinal cord and is responsible for your overall motor skill, memory function, and muscle movement.

As you inhale or digest THC into your blood, it makes its trek towards the CB1 receptor group. Once there, it blocks the receptors and forces the neurotransmissions to cease. It's at this moment that you begin to experience short-term memory, a loss of motor skills, and utter relaxation or stimulation.

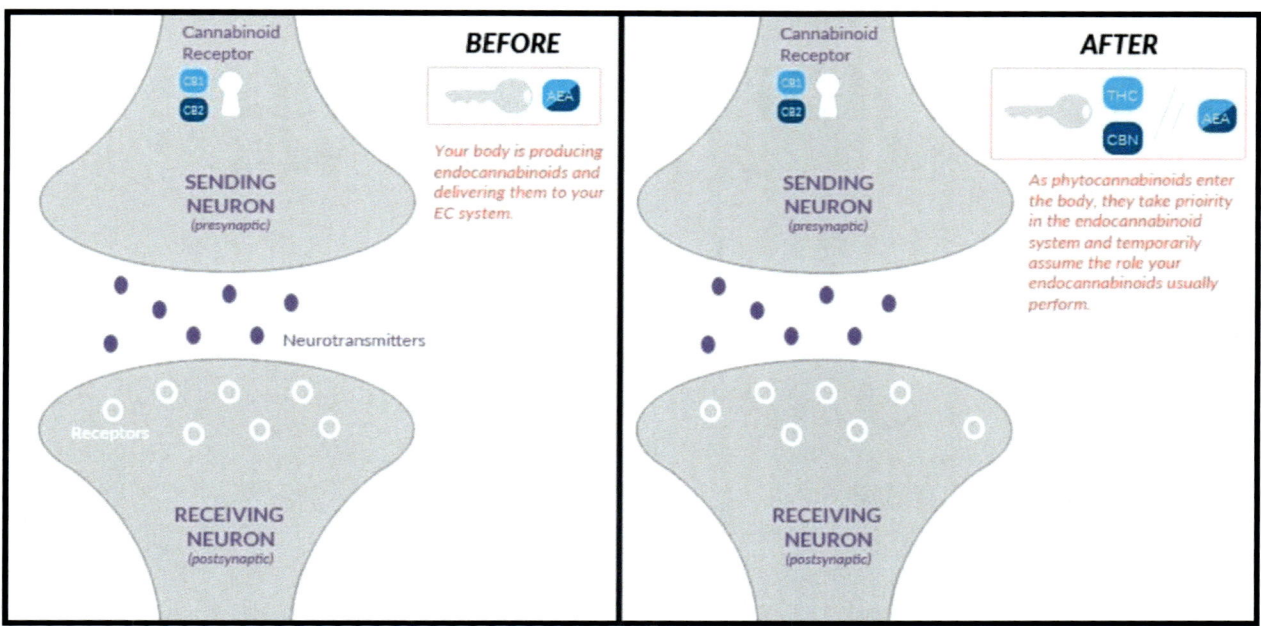

(Shown Above: How THC works in the body. Photo Credits: Key to Cannabis)

How CBD Works in Your Body

Cannabidiol works in a far different manner than THC. CBD is the second most common cannabinoid that's found in cannabis, and the most common cannabinoid found in industrial hemp. CBD is *not* psychoactive and is best known for its medicinal and therapeutic benefits.

CBD was first discovered in 1940 by doctor Roger Adams and his team of researchers. It wasn't until the last decade that meaningful research occurred due to the ongoing prohibition of anything cannabis-related.

As the legalization of marijuana spread, CBD became a popular topic amongst medical professionals that are seeking alternatives to dangerous opioids. It was found that CBD posts a massive pedigree of use-cases. The cherry on top for advocates and researchers was the fact that CBD can be extracted from hemp (a cannabis subspecies). Hemp naturally contains a significant amount of CBD and less than 0.3% THC.

Now, cannabidiol works in your body by triggering *other* proteins and compounds, that in turn, trigger the CB2 receptor group. This may sound confusing at first, but it's necessary to understand how CBD works inside your body.

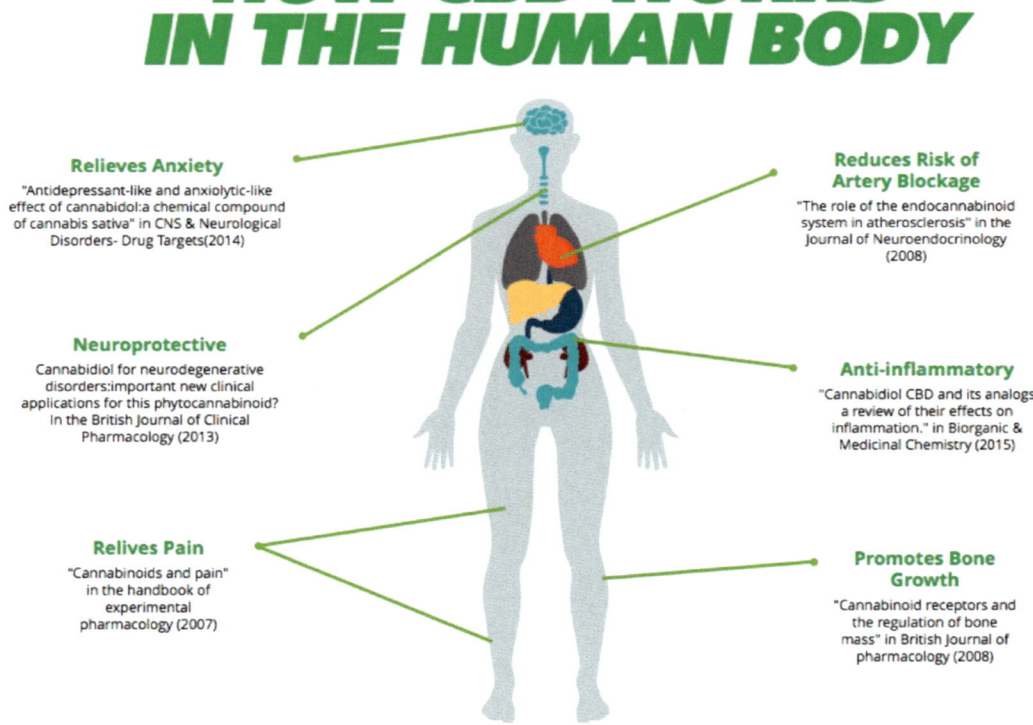

(Shown Above: How CBD works in the body. Photo Credits: HempWorx)

CBD's Commute Into Your Body

Once you consume CBD, it immediately storms a transportation compound, also known as the fatty acid-binding protein (FABP). The FABP acts as an elevator to the molecular level of your body. It's here that anything on board can access your body on the molecular level, and it's at this level that CBD and all other cannabinoids *must* access to take effect.

The extraordinary aspect of the CBD is that once it binds to the FABP, it excludes all other cannabinoids from entering. This technique allows CBD to allow as much of itself into the FABP as possible.

CBD and Pain Management

Once inside your body at the molecular level, CBD begins to take effect all throughout your system. One of the primary compounds that CBD triggers is the TRPV1 protein. The transient receptor potential vanilloid protein is responsible for pain management and the overall immune system.

By activating the TRPV1 protein, CBD creates a cascade effect of relief throughout the body. Inflammation is reduced and pain is decreased. The TRPV1 protein isn't always turned on, and this is why CBD is an invaluable tool to activate it.

It's also believed that the TRPV1 protein sends signals to the CB2 receptor group. By triggering multiple systems that control pain management, CBD effectively reduces chronic pain and inflammation.

CBD and Allosteric Modulation

Another important relationship of CBD is its role as an allosteric modulator. An allosteric modulator is a compound that can change the size or binding capability of a receptor. In this case, CBD has the inherent ability to change the size of CB1 and CB2 receptors to block THC molecules from binding.

What does this mean? It means that if THC is already in your system, CBD will alter receptors and THC will be forced off or won't be able to bind at all. This is why CBD is known to counter the effects of CBD.

CBD and Non-Cannabinoid Receptors

Aside from cannabinoid receptors, CBD has a direct effect on PPARs (peroxisome proliferator-activated receptors). PPARs are believed to be dormant, but once triggered by CBD, they become active. PPARs have been studied to contain neuroprotective, analgesic, anti-tumor, anti-inflammatory, and neuro-functional properties. By understanding the vast network of effects that CBD has on your body, you'll be better equipped to make a decision on which strain is best for you.

Terpenes and Their Role with CBD and THC

As you know, terpenes are organic compounds that are responsible for the aroma and flavor of different strains. They are also known to produce specific recreational and medicinal effects that were once thought to be the result of THC or CBD.

Although research is ongoing, it's been studied that high concentrations of terpenes are responsible for a larger therapeutic index. This means that the higher the terpene concentration, the more effective your cannabis strain will be in delivering medicinal or therapeutic qualities.

When you observe the terpene concentration analysis, you can see which terpene is dominant. Once you view the dominant terpene, you can look up its attributes. For example, myrcene is known to exhibit a strong sedative effect. It's no coincidence that the majority of indica strains contain a high amount of myrcene concentration. Alternatively, limonene is commonly found in sativa strains and is known to elevate the mood and increase energy.

The Necessity of Lab Tested Strains

Now that you understand *how* THC, CBD, and terpenes affect your body, it's time to take this knowledge and turn it into action. When you visit a local marijuana dispensary, you should *only* buy marijuana products that are entirely lab tested.

This means each cannabis strain should show results for:

- THC concentration
- CBD concentration
- Strain Lineage
- Terpene analysis
- Residual chemical analysis
- Bacteria/mold analysis

As you look at these results, you can easily predict the effects of the given THC and CBD levels. For example, Master Kush is rated at 24% THC and 0.8% CBD. You also view that the most abundant terpene is myrcene. From this knowledge, you can assume that Master Kush will produce a strong psychoactive high that will likely result in heavy couch-lock effects.

It's imperative that you shop at marijuana dispensaries that lab tests their strains. This knowledge empowers your decision-making and promotes consumer safety. There's nothing worse than consuming a cannabis strain that negatively affects you.

Before lab testing, countless cannabis consumers were left with marijuana strains that left them feeling paranoid or lazy. The days of unknown weed are behind us, and it's crucial to take advantage of information to make a well-informed decision.

What You Can Expect From a CBD Dominant Cannabis Strain

When you find a 20:1 (CBD: THC) strain, you can already predict how it'll affect you. Since CBD reduces the binding capability of THC, you won't feel the psychoactive effects associated with THC. Instead, you'll feel the therapeutic benefits that are contained within the CBD molecule.

What are the typical effects associated with CBD? Let's take a look.

- Anti-depression
- Anti-anxiety
- Anti-insomnia
- Anti-nausea
- Anti-tumor
- Anti-cancer

- Increased relaxation
- Relief from mental disorders
- Relief from physical disorders

The list of benefits from CBD is extensive, but research has shown that using CBD can significantly decrease the symptoms that you're experiencing from mental or physical issues. ADHD, MS, Alzheimer's, epilepsy, bipolar disorder, acne, glaucoma, anxiety, and so much more can all be helped by using CBD.

Although CBD isn't a cure, it will help relieve a wide variety of issues when used as a daily supplement.

When purchasing cannabis strains for CBD, it's crucial to find the THC and CBD concentration easily. Once you've located the CBD concentration, you can quickly compare it to the THC ratio to make a decision. If you're seeking a high-CBD strain, you won't want to purchase a strain that contains a ratio of 2:28 (2% CBD: 28% THC).

What You Can Expect From a High THC Cannabis Strain

When searching for a high THC cannabis strain, you can easily predict what to expect by viewing these four things: THC concentration, lineage, terpene concentration, and CBD concentration.

First, what's the THC concentration? This critical piece of information will tell you most of what you need to know. Most marijuana strains contain between 14-22% THC, with incredibly potent varieties ranging between 23-35% THC. Strains that have a high amount of THC will last longer than less potent varieties, as well as produce a strong psychoactive effect.

Although the THC concentration will give you an idea of how *strong* a strain is - it doesn't tell you *how* it'll affect you. Strains are categorized into sativas, indicas, and hybrids due to their *lineage* - essentially a strains' parents.

When a pure indica mother and a pure indica father produce offspring, the resulting strain is likely going to exhibit strong indica traits. When a sativa mother and a sativa father produce their offspring, the new strain will likely have strong sativa effects.

In other words, you can have a sativa strain and an indica strain that contain the same THC level but will produce entirely different effects. This scenario becomes further complicated when you introduce hybrids into the scene.

A hybrid is when you cross an indica mother with a sativa father (or vice versa). The result is a hybrid strain that contains characteristics from its indica and sativa lineage. Depending on the outcome, the hybrid may lean more towards its sativa side or indica side.

So, to truly predict the effects of a high THC cannabis strain, you'll need to know the cannabinoid content, terpene content, and lineage. By knowing these details, you'll be able to accurately gauge the potential effects of a given strain. If you don't have lab results at your fingertips, this entire method falls apart.

Knowledge is Power

By understanding the information from this article, you'll have a trove of knowledge to help you make an important decision. When you're searching for something more from a cannabis strain, you'll need to use lab results to make a well-informed decision. This is why you must shop at a marijuana dispensary that carries lab-tested strains. Once you view the available results of your preferred strains, you can enjoy cannabis for its wide-ranging benefits.

POP QUIZ

Question #1: This means that the (BLANK) the terpene concentration, the more effective your cannabis strain will be in delivering medicinal or therapeutic qualities.

Answer: _____

Question #2: Most marijuana strains contain between (BLANK) THC, with incredibly potent varieties ranging between (BLANK) THC.

Answer: _____

Question #3: (BLANK) is the second most common cannabinoid that's found in cannabis, and the most common cannabinoid found in industrial hemp.

Answer: _____

Popular Cannabinoids and How they Affect You...

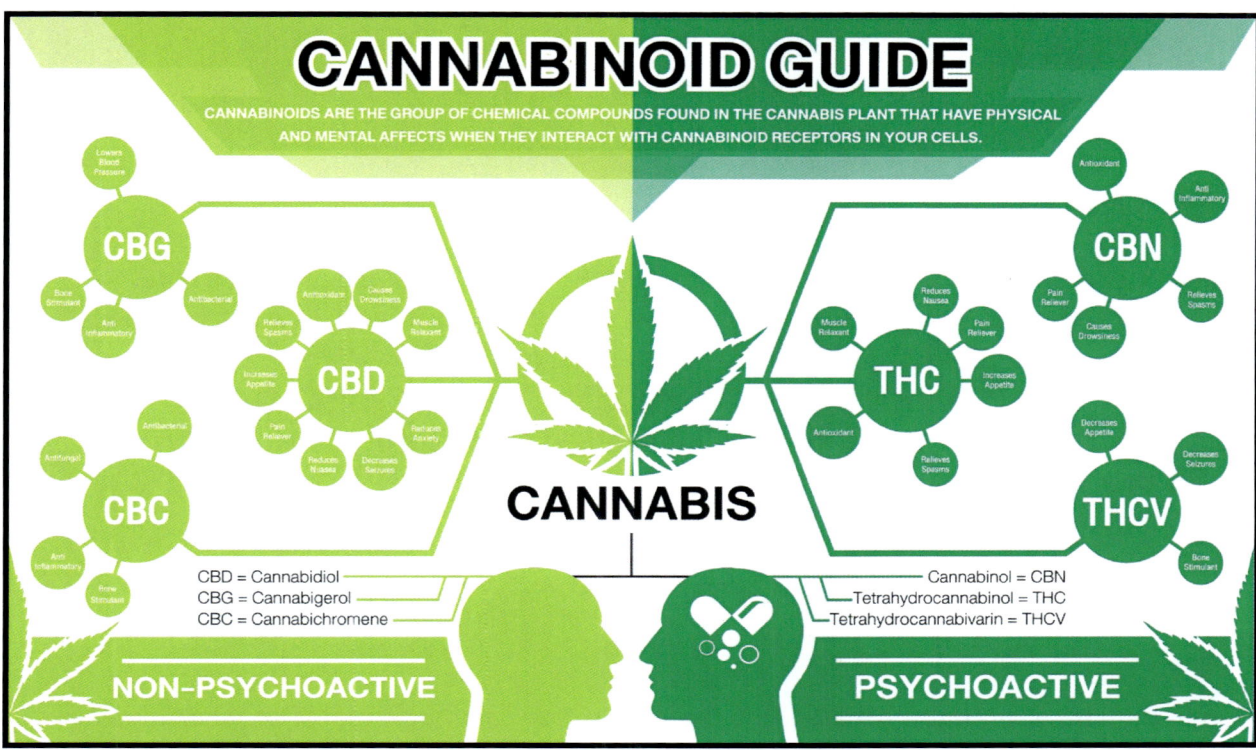

(Shown Above: Cannabinoid Effects.)

The endocannabinoid system in the human body is a naturally occurring system that regulates a variety of physiological processes such as mood, memory and appetite. If a disability or other deficiency occurs, it can often lead to illness.

When cannabis is taken, cannabinoids immediately bind to the most commonly detected endocannabinoid receptors in the brain and immune system. The effects on the human body depend on the specific receptors to which they bind. For example, CBN or cannabinol binds specifically to CB-2 receptors. Depending on the ratio of the absorbed cannabinoids, they have different effects on the body.

Cannabis produces a variety of compounds called cannabinoids, many of which have not been detected in any other plant. How much exactly? It's difficult to say. You will often see people reporting that there are dozens, if not more than 100 cannabis-derived herbal cannabinoids. But it is difficult to know the exact number. Most of them are present in very low concentrations, especially in commercial cannabis products, which prevents scientists from accurately recognizing them. The important point is that there are many. Let's take a closer look at some of the popular cannabinoids found in cannabis products and how they affect us.

Listed Below Are Some Of The Popular Cannabinoids And Their Effect...

THCA (Tetrahydrocannabinolic Acid)

Delta 9 THC is probably the best-known cannabinoid. When people talk about "increasing height," they are referring to the experience of the psychoactive effects of THC. THC starts as THCA, tetrahydrocannabinolic acid, which is one of the popular cannabinoids most commonly found in cannabis. When THCA is heated and converted to THC, it binds to CB1 receptors in the brain and produces psychoactive effects. THC is the only known cannabinoid that causes a psychoactive reaction and may have high therapeutic benefits.

The effect of THCA to the body

Early studies suggested that it could be inert, since THCA is unable to cross the blood-brain barrier and bind to the usual endocannabinoid receptors (CB1 and CB2) like THC and CBD. However, it is known that it works mainly by inhibiting cyclooxygenase enzymes (COX) and other compounds specific for the treatment of inflammation in the body, as well as by acting on TRPA1 receptors (which are responsible for the modulation) the reaction due to pain and itching).

Although CBD also has anti-inflammatory properties, they act through various biological processes. This has led some advocates to refer to THCA as a superior anti-inflammatory agent, but as long as the pathways and direct modes of action are not better understood, it is probably better to say that they are both powerful and different.

(Shown Above: Tetrahydrocannabinolic Acid molecule. Photo Credits: Wikipedia)

CBDA (Cannabidiolic Acid)

CBDA, like THCA, is also one of the popular cannabinoids and also a major constituent of high CBD cannabis. CBDA selectively inhibits the COX-2 enzyme and contributes to the anti-inflammatory effect of cannabis.

CBDA, cannabidiolic acid, is very common in the cannabis plant and becomes CBD on heating. Preclinical studies show that CBDA is a potent antiemetic. An antiemetic is used to treat vomiting and nausea and is often used to reduce the side effects of opioids or chemotherapy.

The effect of CBDA to the body

Rather than relying on the activation of cannabinoid receptors, CBDA interferes with the human endocannabinoid system by modifying the efficacy of four major functions: COX-1 release, COX-2 inhibition, TNF-alpha inhibition, and interleukin-10 release , In the end, these cannabinoids actively support your body's ability to reduce inflammation, improve immune system performance, and significantly lower overall pain levels. Although the actual efficacy of THCA and CBDA is still under investigation, the use of these acidic cannabinoids in the modern cannabis industry is very promising and worthy of investigation by cannabis researchers and processors.

(Shown Above: Cannabidiolic Acid Synthase molecule. Photo Credits: Wikipedia)

CBD (cannabinoids)

CBD has enormous medical potential and also a popular cannabinoids. This is especially true when the right ratio of CBD to THC is used to treat a particular disease. CBD acts as a CB1 and CB2 receptor antagonist but has low binding affinity for both. This suggests that the mechanism of action of CBD is mediated by other brain and body receptors.

The effect of CBD to the body

CBD is one of the popular 120 compounds known as cannabinoids. Many plants contain cannabinoids, but humans usually bind them to cannabis. Unlike other cannabinoids such as tetrahydrocannabinol (THC), CBD does not cause a "high" or psychoactive euphoric effect. In fact, CBD does not affect the same receptors as THC. It also helps to regulate functions such as sleep, immune system reactions and pain.

CBD is a completely different compound than THC and its effects are very complex. It is not psychoactive, that is, it does not produce a "high" effect or alter a person's state of mind, but it does encourage the body to use its effects more effectively.

According to a study published in Neurotherapeutics, this is because CBD makes only a very small contribution to ECS. Instead, it activates or inhibits other compounds in the endocannabinoid system. For example, CBD prevents the body from absorbing anandamide, a compound associated with pain regulation. Thus, increasing the level of anandamide in the blood can relieve the pain.

CBD may also limit inflammation of the brain and nervous system, which may be beneficial for people with pain, insomnia and certain immune system reactions.

(Shown Above: Cannabidiol molecule. Photo Credits: Wikipedia)

CBGA (Cannabigerolic acid)

Cannabigerolic acid is also a popular compound of cannabinoids and also a precursor to one of the three main cannabinoid lines: THCA, CBDA and CBCA. CBGA is the chemical compound of THC and CBD. Enzymes direct it to one of these lines before the heat changes it into different forms.

CBGA appears to act as a weak affinity antagonist for the body's CB1 receptor, making the body more susceptible to cannabinoids in cannabis. The researchers continue to study CBGA to see if it also affects the body's CB2 receptors.

The production of cannabigerolic acid is a unique feature of the cannabis plant. Most medical marijuana strains have CBGA levels that are not rapidly converted to other cannabinoids. However, heating the marijuana plant material, a process known as decarboxylation, helps the CBGA acid to rapidly convert to CBD, which the body can easily use.

CBGA-rich strains easily convert to usable CBD. Industrial hemp seems to have a higher CBGA content than other varieties or varieties of marijuana plants. It is thought that the high levels of CBGA in hemp are due to a recessive gene that is not so common in other plants or cannabis strains.

The effects of CBGA to the body

Unlike other cannabinoids such as tetrahydrocannabinol (THC), CBGA causes no psychoactive effects if swallowed. The researchers believe that CBGA could treat certain types of cancer and schizophrenia. It has also been shown to reduce inflammation, improve bone growth and slow down certain types of bacterial growth.

CBGA can relieve inflammation and relieve pain. Inflammation is a defense mechanism; the body's response to damage or irritants. This is important because inflammation is the fact that the body is actively trying to cure a perceived danger such as a bacterial infection, injury or food allergy.

(Shown Above: Cannabigerolic Acid molecule. Photo Credits: Wikipedia)

CBG (cannabigerolic)

CBG is also one of the popular cannabinoids, it is also present in low concentrations (usually less than 1%) in most cannabis strains, CBG is considered a minor cannabinoid. Surprisingly, however, THC and CBD started as CBG, it is the chemical compound of THC and CBD. Cannabis plants produce cannabigerolic acid (CBGA), the precursor of the three main cannabinoid lines: tetrahydrocannabinolic acid (THCA), cannabidiolic acid (CBDA) and cannabichromoenanic acid (ACSA).

Specific enzymes in the plant break down the CBGA and "direct" it to one of the three lines. The acids are exposed to ultraviolet light or heat and are now becoming the cannabinoids we know: THC and CBD. In most strains CBGA is immediately converted to THCA or CBDA. Thus, more THC means less CBG and CBD (and vice versa) due to the nature of the synthesis of these compounds.

Effects of CBG to the body

Cannabigerolic is considered a minor cannabinoid as it is present in very low concentrations. It is also effective in the treatment of glaucoma because it is a powerful vasodilator, which means it dilates the blood vessels. This increases the blood circulation and supplies the required tissue with oxygen. CBG is promising as an antibacterial, anticancer and potent neuroprotective agent.

(Shown Above: Cannabigerol molecule. Photo Credits: Wikipedia)

CBCA (Cannabichromenic acid)

Cannabichromeninic acid (CBCA) is the acidic version of cannabis chromosomes (CBC) and also a popular cannabinoids. CBCA is a non-psychoactive cannabinoid found in the cannabis plant. It occurs when cannabigerolic acid (CBGA) is broken down. The degradation process occurs when a compound is exposed to heat or ultraviolet light, whereby the parent compound assumes a different molecular structure.

Once created, the CBCA can also undergo the degradation process. Then, cannabinoids such as CBC, cannabicyclol (CBL) and cannabicyclic acid (CBLA) are formed. This fact demonstrates the importance of CBCA for medical cannabis. If CBCA was not broken down, there would not be many useful cannabinoids today.

Effects of CBCA to the body

Although there have not been many studies on the effects of CBCA on the human body at the time of discovery, research is beginning to increase. It has recently been discovered that CBCA has anti-inflammatory properties, a fact that could help many people with inflammatory conditions such as arthritis.

It has also been shown that CBCA is an antifungal that can be helpful in treating a variety of problems such as ringworm, candidiasis and even athlete's foot. There is still much to research about CBCA.

It is important that more researches is done on CBCA before it is used as an alternative medicine. A 2006 study found that CBCA has potential to fight cancer. Better yet, we know that CBC is the second best cannabinoid to reduce or stop the growth of new cancer cells.

CBC naturally enhances the body's endocannabinoids to promote good health and wellbeing. This fact may be responsible for certain anticancer properties. If researchers thought this was true for CBCA, it could be a new robust and life-saving treatment for patients undergoing treatment for a variety of cancers. However, it is important to understand that CBCA requires much more research before it can be used in this way. The legalization of marijuana will open up more opportunities for researchers who want to study less well-understood cannabinoids such as the CBCA.

(Shown Above: Cannabichromenic molecule. Photo Credits: Wikipedia)

CBC (Cannabichromene)

Cannabichromene or CBC is also a popular cannabinoids that does not attract much praise or attention, but has shown profound benefits. Similar to cannabidiol (CBD) and tetrahydrocannabinol (THC), CBC is derived from cannabigerolic acid (CBGA). From there, the enzymes convert it to carboxylic acid cannabichromene (CBCA). In this case of CBCA it goes through the CBC synthase (the enzymes that trigger the specific process). Over time, or when exposed to heat, the CBCA disintegrates into cannabis bromide, a process called decarboxylation.

The effect of CBC to the body

CBC is not intoxicating and therefore does not produce a euphoric effect like THC. The reason why it is not intoxicating is that it does not go well with CB1 cannabinoid receptors in the brain. However, CBC binds to other receptors in the body, such as the vanilloid receptor 1 (TRPV1) and the transient receptor potential ankyrin 1 (TRPA1), both of which are associated with pain perception. , When CBC activates these receptors, higher levels of natural endocannabinoids such as anandamide are released.

While CBC offers undeniable benefits, researchers also believe it seems to work in synergy with other cannabinoids, a term known as the entourage effect. This effect of cooperation between THC and CBD is well known, but it is not known if other cannabinoids have an impact on the environment.

(Shown Above: Cannabigerol molecule. Photo Credits: Wikipedia)

CBN (Cannabinol)

Cannabinol or CBN is a popular cannabinoids, it is also known to degrade tetrahydrocannabinol (THC) over time due to exposure to oxygen, ultraviolet light or heat. After decomposition, CBN becomes only slightly psychoactive, resulting in little or no psychoactive effects. The fact that this cannabinoid is not very psychoactive does not mean that it is not powerful.

CBN / cannabinol is a cannabinoid, that is, it is one of the active ingredients of marijuana. These are the compounds that make marijuana behave the way it is in the brain and in the body.

CBN is a minor cannabinoid, which means that unlike THC and CBD, it is not initially present in high concentrations of marijuana. However, the way marijuana creates CBN allows this little actor to truly differentiate himself from others.

The effects of CBN to the body

CBN offers a unique profile of effects and benefits to the body that encourages researchers to engage in more advanced scientific research. CBN is the strongest cannabinoid that has been identified to promote sleep, making CBN-rich cannabis an ideal treatment for insomnia. Indica strains seem to have more CBN than Sativa strains, which would explain the widespread belief that Indicas make you sleepy and give you a high. According to Steep Hill Labs, 5 mg CBN is as effective as the 10 mg dose of Diazepam, a mild pharmaceutical tranquilizer. For those people who rely on cannabis for a night of filming, a little CBN might be helpful. CBN is a CB2 and CB1 receptor agonist (a chemical that binds to and activates a receptor to produce a biological response).

(Shown Above: Cannabinol molecule. Photo Credits: Wikipedia)

THCV (tetrahydrocannabivarin)

As the name implies, THCV resembles THC in terms of molecular structure and psychoactive properties and it is also a popular cannabinoids, but offers a variety of distinct and very different effects. Note for the evaporation process: THCV has a boiling point of 220 ° C (428 ° F). You must increase it to a higher THC value.

For many, THCV looks very similar to THC in appearance and appearance. Although THC and THCV have some similarities, they are also very different, especially in terms of the impact they have on cannabis users. How does THCV resemble THC? On the one hand, these cannabinoids are very similar in their chemical structure. However, the manufacturing process of these two cannabinoids is very different.

In other words, THCV goes through a process that converts it into cannabigerovaric acid (CBGVA). Subsequently, CBGVA decomposes into the carboxylic acid tetrahydrocannabivarin (THCVA). From there, THCVA can undergo a decarboxylation process using UV light or heat to produce THCV.

In addition, THC and THCV activate certain receptors in our body. These main receptors are called CB1 and CB2. THC and THCV have an effect on the same receptors, but it is important to know that this reaction acts as a CB1 and CB2 receptor antagonist. Since THCV is a CB1 and CB2 receptor antagonist, it means that THCV blocks THC, thereby preventing cannabis users from feasting.

The effects of THVC to the body

THCV or tetrahydrocannabivarin is a cannabis compound that offers a unique set of effects and medicinal benefits that set it apart from other cannabinoids such as THC and CBD. Whether you are a patient under the influence of medical marijuana looking for a certain relief or as an occasional consumer looking for a specific effect, the THVC is a fascinating combination that certainly beats many waves in the world cannabis with its full potential.

(Shown Above: Tetrahyrdocannabivarin molecule. Photo Credits: Wikipedia)

CBDV (Cannabidivarin)

Cannabidivarin is a CBD homologue and one of the most popular cannabinoid compounds, which means that they have a similar structure. In fact, cannabidivarin like CBD has 7 double bond isomers and 30 stereoisomers. There is a side chain that is shortened by two methylene bridges.

Another similarity that cannabidivarin shares with CBD is the fact that both are not psychoactive. Thus, anxious patients who are sensitive to high levels of THC may still take advantage of some benefits without causing the triggering effect of panic.

It is not common to find cannabidivarin in strains that you would encounter in a clinic. Strains with higher CBD levels also tend to be richer in CBDV. Today, most strains are bred for a high THC and terpene level.

CBDV or cannabidivarin also comes from cannabis and hemp plants. These molecules, commonly known as cannabinoids, are responsible in part for the many therapeutic effects and benefits of cannabis.

The effects of CBDV on the body

Much of CBDV research has focused on the impact on seizures. GW Pharmaceuticals, the first FDA-approved CBD drug, Epidiolex, is actively developing a CBDV-based drug known as GPW42006 to reduce or prevent seizures and the like.

Research has shown that CBDV influences the neurochemical pathway of capsaicin receptors involved in the onset as well as the progression of multiple types of epilepsy. GW reports that CBDV has demonstrated antiepileptic results in a number of in vitro and in vivo epilepsy models.

(Shown Above: Cannabidivarin molecule. Photo Credits: Wikipedia)

Verdict

Cannabinoids are widely known for their antiepileptic, anti-inflammatory, nausea, antifungal, and anticancer effects, and science has scratched the surface. The extent to which these effects are expressed is the result of the environmental effect. The effect of the follow-up is that cannabinoids work better together than on their own. THC and CBD cause stronger healing properties, which differ depending on the concentration and presence of other cannabinoids. In addition, terpenes, the oils that give the scent its cannabis fragrance, in combination with cannabinoids contribute to the therapeutic effects of the plant on the body. The strong combination of these natural chemicals leads to the medical effects that have made cannabis its reputation as a medicinal agent.

When it comes to the definition of cannabinoids and their chemical bases, it is not very difficult to determine their purpose. These are compound medicinal compounds derived from the cannabis plant, mainly from their buds. The human body on the other hand produce the same chemicals called endocannabinoids. When people consume cannabis, the compounds in the plant attach themselves to the CB1 and CB2 receptors in our brain and body.

Cannabis has the power to alter the regulation of homeostasis, a process that balances different systems in our body. The researchers not only discovered that our body has cannabinoids, but also a complete endocannabinoid system that contains cannabinoids. In this way, humans can use the compounds contained in nature and in the cannabis plant.

Up to 100 different types of cannabinoids have been isolated so far, but THC has been described as the primary chemical in cannabis due to its psychoactive effect. This is one of the reasons why scientists continue to research this plant and find possible remedies for many diseases.

References

https://www.leafly.com/news/cannabis-101/list-major-cannabinoids-cannabis-effects

https://citiva.com/types-of-cannabinoids/

https://ionizationlabs.com/what-is-cannabichromenic-acid-cbca/

https://www.cerilliant.com/shopOnline/Item_Details.aspx?itemno=028d0e2d-2f32-4770-acfc-dd89a5df9ce3&item=C-150-1ML

Ingest or Inhale? 5 Differences Between Cannabis Edibles and Flower...

(Shown Above: Flower vs Edibles. Photo Credits: Leafly)

When it comes to deciding between cannabis edibles and marijuana flower, It's always a challenging choice. Read along to learn the 5 differences between cannabis edibles and flower to make your indecision a thing of the past.

Difference in Absorption

The most significant difference between cannabis-infused food and dried flowers is the *absorption rate*. This rate is directly affected by the way that the THC is absorbed into your blood.

When you smoke cannabis, you're combusting the flower and activating the THC through a process called decarboxylation. This process turns the inactive THC-A into the psychoactive THC form. The cannabis smoke that you inhale is filled with activated THC, which fills your lungs and finds its way into your blood. This entire process happens quickly, and you'll feel the effects of THC within seconds.

When you ingest cannabis edibles, the process is drastically different. The THC within edibles need to reach your blood to take effect, but it must first be digested. Typically, cannabis edibles can take anywhere from 1-3 hours to take full effect. The THC must travel through your digestive tract, and once there, it passes through the lining of the stomach to reach the blood.

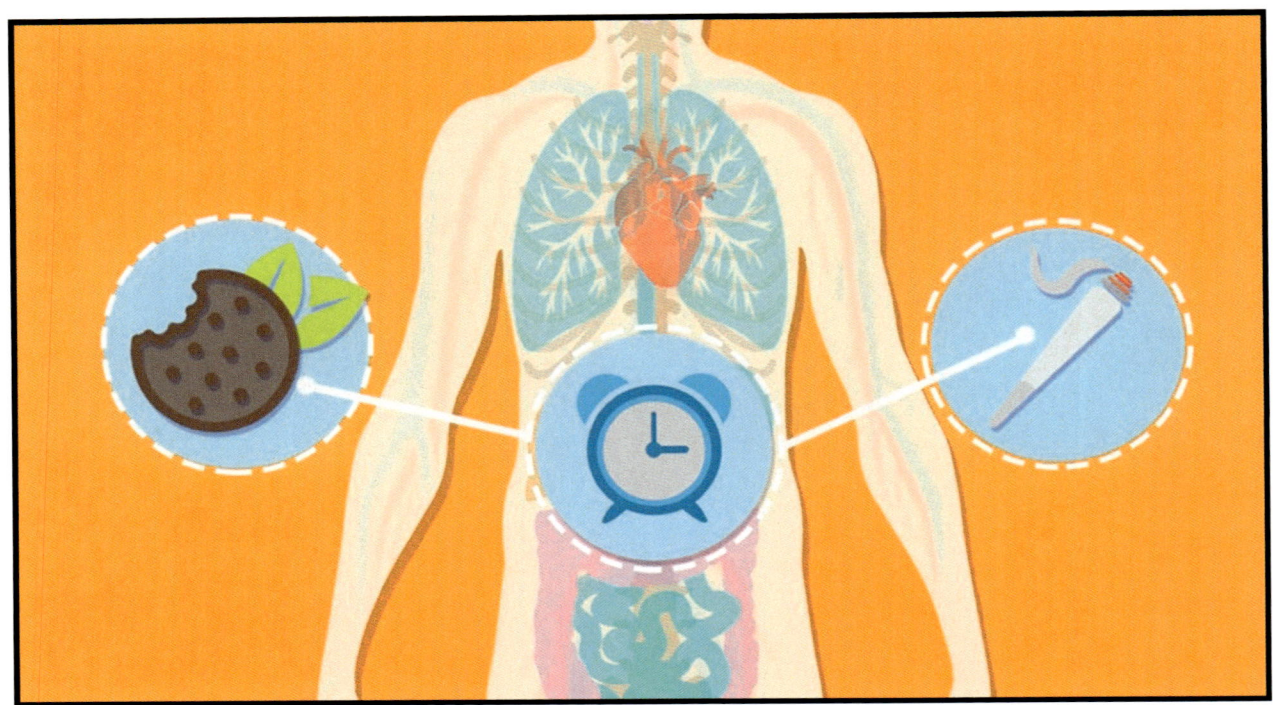

(*Shown Above: Flower vs Edibles. Photo Credits: Green Solution*)

The Duration and Effects

Once the THC is absorbed from dried flowers or cannabis edibles, the results will vary drastically.

The duration and effects of cannabis edibles are much stronger compared to smoking flowers. Although the dosage plays a significant role in this, it's known that edibles last far longer. On average, most users that experience cannabis edibles are high from 3-8 hours - with some extended effects lasting an eye-popping 16 hours.

The effects of edibles are similar to those of smoking flowers - but on steroids. It's for this reason that many advocate for starting with incredibly small doses when it comes to using edibles. By doing so, you won't take to much and become overwhelmed by the potent effects of marijuana edibles.

The effects and duration of smoking cannabis flowers are potent - yet last far shorter compared to edibles. Cannabis flowers typically test between 16-22% THC, which, when smoked, will leave most users feeling high for 1-2 hours. The apex of the high doesn't typically last much longer than 30-minutes, but high THC strains could influence a much stronger sensation.

Gauging Potency

When it comes to cannabis edibles and marijuana flowers, it can be challenging to gauge the potency of each product. Although cannabis has become legalized for medicinal or recreational purposes in many states, it's still common to purchase marijuana from illegal dispensaries. These dispensaries don't a lab test their products, which makes it far more difficult (and dangerous) to gauge the potency of a given cannabis product.

Marijuana edibles are notorious for not containing THC content on their packaging, which makes it difficult to consume the perfect amount. Due to the lengthy time it takes for cannabis edibles to digest, you may end up feeling too high or not high enough. This, in effect, is a potential waste of time, which is why it's crucial that you always seek cannabis edibles that are lab tested and professionally packaged.

Although you should never buy cannabis flowers that aren't lab tested, many still do. Purchasing cannabis flowers that haven't been tested are less difficult to gauge when compared with edibles. The effects of smoking cannabis flowers are nearly instant, and you'll know precisely how strong or weak a strain is within a few minutes.

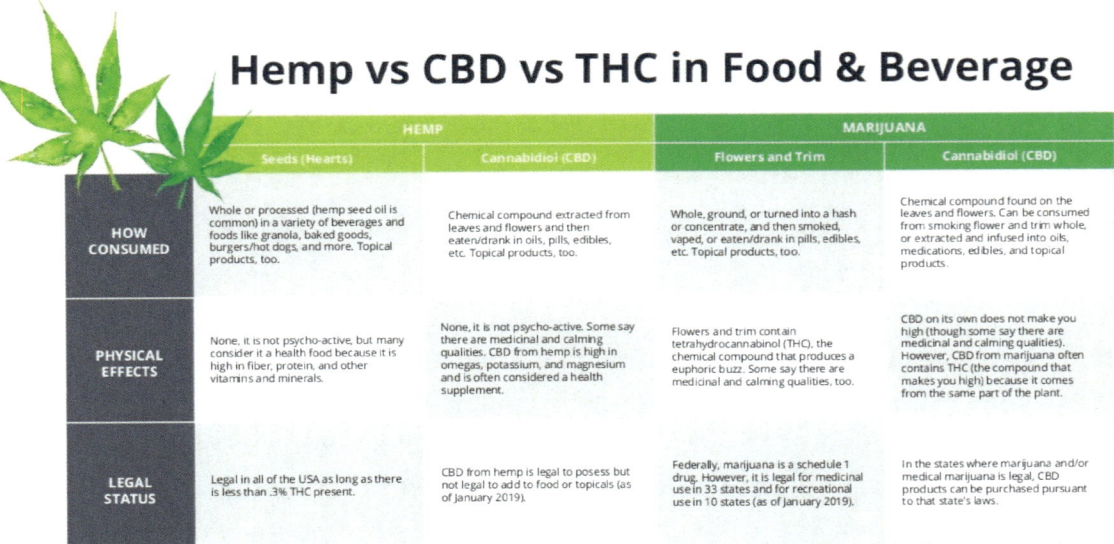

Hemp vs CBD vs THC in Food & Beverage

	HEMP		MARIJUANA	
	Seeds (Hearts)	Cannabidiol (CBD)	Flowers and Trim	Cannabidiol (CBD)
HOW CONSUMED	Whole or processed (hemp seed oil is common) in a variety of beverages and foods like granola, baked goods, burgers/hot dogs, and more. Topical products, too.	Chemical compound extracted from leaves and flowers and then eaten/drank in oils, pills, edibles, etc. Topical products, too.	Whole, ground, or turned into a hash or concentrate, and then smoked, vaped, or eaten/drank in pills, edibles, etc. Topical products, too.	Chemical compound found on the leaves and flowers. Can be consumed from smoking flower and trim whole, or extracted and infused into oils, medications, edibles, and topical products.
PHYSICAL EFFECTS	None, it is not psycho-active, but many consider it a health food because it is high in fiber, protein, and other vitamins and minerals.	None, it is not psycho-active. Some say there are medicinal and calming qualities. CBD from hemp is high in omegas, potassium, and magnesium and is often considered a health supplement.	Flowers and trim contain tetrahydrocannabinol (THC), the chemical compound that produces a euphoric buzz. Some say there are medicinal and calming qualities, too.	CBD on its own does not make you high (though some say there are medicinal and calming qualities). However, CBD from marijuana often contains THC (the compound that makes you high) because it comes from the same part of the plant.
LEGAL STATUS	Legal in all of the USA as long as there is less than .3% THC present.	CBD from hemp is legal to posess but not legal to add to food or topicals (as of January 2019).	Federally, marijuana is a schedule 1 drug. However, it is legal for medicinal use in 33 states and for recreational use in 10 states (as of January 2019).	In the states where marijuana and/or medical marijuana is legal, CBD products can be purchased pursuant to that state's laws.

Disclaimer: Food & Drink Resources (FDR) does not promote, condone, or advocate drug use. FDR cannot be held responsible for material on its website pages or pages we provide links to that promote illegal activities.

(Shown Above: Hemp vs CBD vs THC in Foods. Photo Credits: Food & Drink Resources)

The Difficulty of Dosing Edibles

A primary difference between smoking marijuana flowers and cannabis edibles is the fact that edibles are difficult to dose. For most, properly dosing edibles is filled with trial and error. Rarely do users find the perfect dose in one try. Due to the prolonged amount of time that it takes for edibles to take effect, users must wait for hours to gauge the effects. You may wait for 3 hours, only to find that the dose was far too weak - or vice versa.

The Healthier Alternative

Many ask: "what's the healthiest way to consume cannabis?" This question has spurred many debates, but it's apparent that edibles are far healthier than smoking cannabis flowers.

The reason why cannabis edibles are the healthiest option is that they don't require you to smoke. Smoking anything is considered damaging to your lungs, whether it's cannabis or tobacco. For this reason, many medical patients are unable to smoke, which means their only alternative is to eat it.

Which is Right For You?

Now that you understand 5 of the most significant differences between cannabis edibles and marijuana flowers, which is right for you? There is no clear winner, but rather, only your personal preference.

POP QUIZ

Question #1: (BLANK) is probably the best-known cannabinoid.

Answer: _____

Question #2: The most significant difference between cannabis-infused food and dried flowers is the (BLANK).

Answer: _____

Question #3: On average, most users that experience cannabis edibles are high from 3-8 hours - with some extended effects lasting an eye-popping (BLANK) hours.

Answer: _____

Question #4: (BLANK) is the strongest cannabinoid that has been identified to promote sleep, making (BLANK)-rich cannabis an ideal treatment for insomnia.

Answer: _____

Question #5: (BLANK) appears to act as a weak affinity antagonist for the body's CB1 receptor, making the body more susceptible to cannabinoids in cannabis.

Answer: _____

5 Differences Between Cannabis Concentrates and Flower...

(*Shown Above: Flower vs Concentrates.*)

When you're browsing your local cannabis dispensary for a new product, it's essential to know the difference between two of the most popular products. Cannabis concentrates and dried marijuana flowers are incredibly popular among cannabis enthusiasts, but few understand the significant differences between the two. Join us as we describe the 5 differences between cannabis concentrates and flower.

Terpene Concentration

If you've tried a marijuana extract that has a high concentration of terpenes, then you can attest to the drastic flavor difference compared to dried cannabis flowers. If you've never tried a cannabis concentrate, then read carefully.

Cannabis concentrates are precisely that - *concentrated* forms of cannabis compounds. These compounds consist of cannabinoids, terpenes, and lipids. The vital term, in this case, is terpenes.

Terpenes are organic compounds that are responsible for the flavor and aroma of the majority of plants. Cannabis is within this group, and cannabis enthusiasts can thank these incredible compounds for the mouth-watering flavors that marijuana exhibits.

In this case, cannabis concentrates have a far higher terpene concentration than dried flowers. Where cannabis flowers may have upwards of a 1-2% terpene concentration, marijuana extracts can have 8-10%. This is a significant difference, and you'll surely notice the difference between marijuana extracts and dried cannabis flowers.

When you indulge in marijuana flowers, you'll only notice a brief flavor. However, cannabis concentrations, such as live resin, allow you to experience the essence of the marijuana strain in concentrated form. It's through marijuana extracts that have driven the rise of terpene connoisseurs.

(*Shown Above: Terp Sauce.*)

Form

Another significant difference between cannabis flowers and marijuana extracts is their form. Although the flowers of cannabis take on different sizes, color, and density - they are still flowers that follow a similar structure.

Marijuana concentrates, on the other hand, take on many different forms. If you've ever looked at the cannabis extract section in your local dispensary, you'll surely find many products that look entirely different.

Cannabis extracts can be liquid, wax, or powder. The various names in the cannabis concentrate family are shatter, crumble, live resin, pull n' snap, and Rick Simpson oil. Each of these has unique characteristics regarding their form - which impacts their overall potency and taste.

Potency

There's no other way to say it: cannabis concentrates are far stronger than marijuana flowers. The highest known THC concentration recorded for a dried flower is 35%. The highest known THC concentration for marijuana extracts is 99%.

Marijuana concentrates are far stronger because this extraction process strips the plant of all of its' cannabinoids. The dominant cannabinoid found in cannabis is THC, which is the psychoactive component in marijuana.

Once the extraction process is complete, the end product contains only THC and terpenes. The marijuana concentrations that contain the highest level of THC tend to be what are known as isolates, which means they only contain THC.

For most users, using cannabis concentrates results in a drastically heightened THC tolerance. This rapid tolerance increase is because of the exposure to large amounts of THC all at once. Users who use dried marijuana flowers have a far slower rate of increasing their THC tolerance when compared with those that use cannabis extracts.

Method of Use

This is a glaring difference between cannabis concentrates and dried marijuana flowers. Although marijuana concentrates and flowers can be used with vaporizers, they differ in every other regard.

Cannabis concentrates are normally dabbed through the use of an oil rig. These bong-like devices allow for incredibly high temperatures to consume marijuana extracts. Small metallic spoons are used to scrape up the sticky oil to place into the dabbing rig. Cannabis flowers, however, are traditionally consumed via glass pipes, bongs, joints, and blunts. A regular lighter is sufficient for dried cannabis flowers, whereas torch-like lighters are specifically used for cannabis concentrates.

For many, the intricacies and cost of a dab rig are enough to steer many away. The learning curve is far higher when it comes to using cannabis concentrates via a dab rig. Specific temperatures, specialized equipment, and the danger of using a blow-torch are commonalities when using cannabis extracts.

Another difference regarding the method of use is that cannabis concentrates can be eaten directly. Marijuana flowers are not immediately psychoactive and must be activated by the use of heat. This method is called decarboxylation, and it's the reaction that's responsible for THC becoming psychoactive.

When it comes to cannabis flowers, all you need is a Bic lighter and rolling papers. For many, this ease of use and simple method is a significant deciding factor.

(Shown Above: Dab Rig (Concentrates).)

Cannabinoids Are Stripped From The Plant

Cannabinoids, usually in the form of THC and CBD, are the primary compounds that are stripped from the marijuana plant when producing cannabis extracts. This is a fundamental difference between cannabis extracts and flower.

Cannabinoids are extracted through the use of chemical solvents or solventless methods. A popular solvent to extract cannabinoids is butane. This chemical solvent is incredibly efficient at stripping the marijuana plant of all its cannabinoids. However, this chemical is also highly dangerous to use.

Solventless extracts are produced by the use of heat, pressure, or water. Concentrates that are derived from solventless methods are typically considered far safer than those that require a solvent.

Marijuana flowers don't undergo further processing after they've been dried and cured. Instead, they become immediately available for consumption once they're done curing. To create a marijuana extract, the extra step of stripping the cannabinoids from the flower is necessitated.

The Deciding Factor

When it comes to choosing cannabis concentrates or marijuana flowers, the deciding factor boils down to personal preference. Not everyone is seeking the highest THC concentrations that marijuana extracts have to offer. On the other hand, there are many who are wholly concerned with the flavor of their marijuana.

Cannabis concentrates and marijuana flowers each offer unique aspects, and it's your personal preference that will lend credence to your decision.

POP QUIZ

Question #1: A popular solvent to extract cannabinoids is (BLANK).

Answer: _____

Question #2: This method is called (BLANK), and it's the reaction that's responsible for THC becoming psychoactive.

Answer: _____

Question #3: Where cannabis flowers may have upwards of a 1-2% terpene concentration, marijuana extracts can have (BLANK).

Answer: _____

The different ways to smoke and consume cannabis...

One of the most important things to consider when it comes to cannabis is the delivery method. The way you consume cannabis affects the way you experience the health benefits and the high.

There are many different cannabis delivery methods, from joints and vaporizers to edibles and oils, and it can be overwhelming to choose between them. Each different method has its advantages and drawbacks, and a delivery method that suits one person might not suit another person.

You'll probably choose your cannabis delivery method based on a few factors, including:

- **Purpose.** Do you want to relax, be social, or treat a specific condition or ailment?
- **Access.** What cannabis delivery method is easier for you to access? If it would be difficult to buy a vaporizer, for example, you might cross that off your list.
- **Cost.** If you're on a budget, what's the cheapest delivery method for you?
- **Timeframe.** Would you like it to have fast-acting effects? How long would you like the effect to last?
- **Health considerations.** If you have a lung condition, for example, you wouldn't opt for smoking.

Here's what you need to know about the most popular cannabis methods.

Joints

A joint is one of the most classic, old-school ways to consume cannabis.

(Shown Right: Hand Rolling Joint.)

Joints are relatively easy to make. All you need is a rolling paper. Joints are also portable and easy to share, which is why they're popular for social smokers. Unfortunately, they have their disadvantages. Because it involves combustion, smoking a joint is not great for your lungs.

Joints sometimes contain a mixture of cannabis and tobacco. These are often called spliffs or blunts. While many people prefer the buzz and taste that comes with combining the two, please remember that nicotine is addictive and tobacco can harm your health.

One huge advantage of smoking cannabis is that it's fast-acting - you feel the effects almost immediately.

Hand Pipes

Pipes are easy to use. You don't need to have any rolling skills to use it - just prepare the weed and pack the pipe. Nowadays, there are many different kinds of pipes, including twisty pipes which can be easier to pack and use. Beautiful glass pipes are often a point of pride for many cannabis enthusiasts.

As with other forms of smoking, it's fast-acting, but it can have negative effects on your lungs.

(Shown Above: Glass Pipe.)

Water Pipes

Water pipes, such as bongs, are also a popular way to smoke cannabis. While they're less portable than joints and hand pipes, bongs are often fun and used for social cannabis consumption. Using water pipes is also a fast-acting cannabis delivery method.

(Shown Right: Cannabis Water Pipe.)

While it's a little less portable and harder to clean than a regular hand pipe or joint, they're still a crowd favorite. Many people feel that the water 'clears' the air of harmful components, which makes it easier on the lungs. Some people feel that they cough less when they use bongs as opposed to pipes or joints. However, there is little science that proves that water pipes are better than hand pipes or joints.

Vaping

Vaping is not considered a 'smoking' method, but rather an 'inhalation' method. This is

because it doesn't involve combustion. Cannabis vaporizers do heat the product, but it's not as rough on your lungs. A 2007 study looked at the self-reported symptoms of vaping, and it found that the respiratory effects of vaping was better than that of smoking. Because it's not rough on the lungs but it's still fast-acting, quite a few cannabis doctors recommend it, and people often prefer it for treating pain.

(Shown Above: Cannabis Vape Rig.)

There are a number of vaporizer products on the market. They range in size and function, from pen vaporizers, which are small and portable, to desktop vaporizers, which usually need to be plugged into an outlet to work.

One tricky thing with vaporizers is that they can be too expensive for a casual user, as opposed to joints or pipes. They also need to be cleaned out and prepared, which can be cumbersome.

Topicals

Topicals are creams, oils, balms, and lotions that are infused with cannabis. They are applied to the skin. They are often combined with other ingredients that soothe the skin or reduce pain.

Topicals are great because they provide localized relief. This means that you can apply it directly to the area you want to treat - if your ankle is sore, for example, you can massage it with the topical treatment and wait for it to work. According to research, cannabinoids can be absorbed by your skin within minutes, producing fast effects.

(Shown Right: Cannabis Topical.)

Topical treatments won't make you high, even if they contain THC. This means that you can continue to work, drive, and function normally without the buzz getting in the way. This is great for people who don't want to feel intoxicated but still need pain relief.

If you have all-over pain, or if you want to treat something like anxiety, topicals aren't the best choice as they can only treat a localized area.

Tinctures and Oils

Tinctures and oils are liquids containing concentrated amounts of cannabinoids. While oils are obviously oil-based, tinctures are alcohol-based. Instead of swallowing these, you drop them under your tongue and keep them there. The cannabinoids absorb into the capillaries in your mouth.

Some tinctures and oils are CBD-only, which is useful if you want the health benefits of CBD without the high. Others contain CBD, THC, and other cannabinoids. When made by a professional company, your tinctures and oils should be clearly marked so that you know the composition, the ingredients, and the strength of the liquid.

Many people prefer using tinctures and oils because, if given in a specific dosage, it's easy to choose exactly how much of each cannabinoid you'll be ingesting. With a little practice and experience, you'll learn how to adjust the dosage exactly to your needs.

(*Shown Above: Cannabis Tinctures & Oil.*)

Edibles

Still a party favorite, cannabis-infused edibles are popular among recreational cannabis users and medical cannabis patients alike.

(*Shown Right: Cannabis Brownies.*)

Edibles are great because they can combine the medical powers of cannabis with a tasty snack. Making your own edibles is pretty simple, but be warned - it's important to measure out your ingredients properly so that your edibles aren't too weak or too strong.

Don't eat too many edibles at once. Because you're digesting the cannabinoids, it takes a while for the high to kick in - usually around thirty minutes - and many people make the mistake of thinking the edibles are weak and overindulging in them. We've all heard stories about people eating too many brownies at college parties!

To make it easier, you can buy edibles that were made by professionals. Often, edibles sold by legitimate companies will be labelled so that you know exactly how strong they are. And your options aren't limited to old-fashioned brownies - you can now buy gummies, candies, savory foods, cakes, chocolate, and more.

Tablets and capsules

Tablets and capsules are an easy, no-nonsense cannabis delivery method. It's very easy to take the exact dosage of cannabinoids you need. Some capsules only contain CBD, but others contain a range of cannabinoids. As with tinctures and oils, this is a really discreet cannabis delivery method - it produces no smell, and you can consume it within seconds.

Cannabis tablets and capsules don't work as fast as smoking does, because they need to be ingested, like edibles. If you buy cannabis tablets or capsules, make sure you're getting it from a reputable brand.

(*Shown Above: Cannabis Pills.*)

Raw Juices

Raw cannabis juice has been a popular trend for quite a few years. It can't get you high - cannabis needs to be heated to do that - but many people claim that it can be a part of a healthy diet. William Courtney, MD, a physician based in California, claims that raw cannabis should be a part of everybody's daily diet. The entirety of the plant can be added to a blender and mixed with water to create a juice.

As with other leafy green plants, cannabis does contain nutrients - many of which are lost when heated. Some people claim that raw cannabis juice has calming and pain-fighting effects, but so far, no scientific research has been conducted on it.

The cannabis delivery method you choose depends on your lifestyle and preferences. The best way to choose one is with a little experimentation. However you ingest it, make sure you're getting top-quality cannabis and cannabis products.

If you're hoping to treat a medical condition with cannabis, it's best to speak to a cannabis-friendly physician beforehand. They should be able to help you figure out which cannabis delivery methods will suit you.

(*Shown Above: Cannabis Juice.*)

POP QUIZ

Question #1: Topical treatments won't make you high, even if they contain (BLANK).

Answer: _____

Question #2: Vaping is not considered a 'smoking' method, but rather an (BLANK) method.

Answer: _____

Question #3: If you have a lung condition, for example, you wouldn't opt for (BLANK).

Answer: _____

Question #4: Some people claim that (BLANK) has calming and pain-fighting effects, but so far, no scientific research has been conducted on it.

Answer: _____

Question #5: The cannabinoids absorb into the (BLANK) in your mouth.

Answer: _____

7 Factors That Affect Your Cannabis High...

Your cannabis high isn't strictly the result of the THC content. Although the percentage of THC plays a significant role, there are many other factors that affect your cannabis high. Join us as we take a look at the 7 factors that affect your cannabis high - and how knowing these will allow you to fine-tune your experience.

#1 THC Content

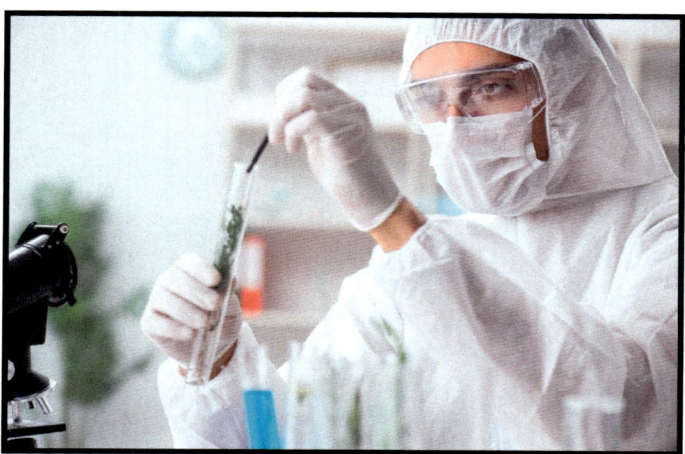

Tetrahydrocannabinol, also known as THC, is a psychoactive cannabinoid. Although it's directly responsible for getting you high, it isn't the sole contributor. It's important to understand that high THC content will affect you significantly more than a strain with a low THC percentage.

(Shown Left: Cannabis Lab Testing.)

A strain that's rated at 32% THC will profoundly affect your experience compared to that of a 12% THC strain. The stronger strain may only take one drag to leave you feeling dazed, whereas the weaker variety may leave you buzzed.

The same thing can be said when comparing a cannabis concentrate that's rated at 99% THC and a bubble hash that contains 40% THC. These products will surely produce different effects that will directly influence your cannabis high.

#2 Method of Consumption

Another significant factor that will affect your cannabis high is how you consume it. Marijuana products come in a wide variety of styles, such as edibles, flowers, concentrates, and vape cartridges.

When you smoke cannabis flowers, you have a plethora of options. Joints, blunts, small pipes, massive bongs, or handheld bubblers all affect your cannabis high. One hit from a 4-foot bong will surely leave you feeling some-type-of-way compared to a small stealth-pipe.

When vaping, you can take incredibly large hits due to the smoothness offered by vape products. When combusting marijuana, the harsh smoke forces you to take smaller hits.

Concentrates are consumed via a hybrid method that contains properties from combusting and vaping. Dab rigs are used to consume concentrates, and this method is known to produce massive hits and dizzying effects.

Edibles are entirely different than the previous three because marijuana-infused food is eaten. Instead of affecting you instantly, edibles take between 1-3 hours to take effect. If you're consuming sublingual edibles, then the time to take effect is reduced to 15-45 minutes.

Therefore, all of these different methods of consumption will result in different highs. The high from an edible is incredibly potent that will last for hours on end. The high produced from a dab rig is incredibly potent but short-lived.

#3 Your Tolerance

Not every stoner is created equal. All jokes aside, your tolerance will play a significant role in affecting your cannabis high.

If you smoke 3 times a day, it's likely that you have a sky-high tolerance. If you've just begun using marijuana, then it's likely that your tolerance is fairly low. However, it's possible that newbies will have a battle-hardened veteran's tolerance and a cannabis connoisseur can only take one hit before becoming too high.

If your cannabis tolerance is too high, it's likely that the effects of THC are short-lived. This will affect your experience because you'll need to consume more to attain certain effects. If you have a low tolerance, then you won't need to use a lot to reach a comfortable high.

Aside from the amount that it takes to get high, the quality of the high is also directly affected by your tolerance. If you have a low tolerance, then you may become frightened when someone passes you a high-THC joint. Since your body isn't accustomed to THC, you may react in a negative way.

#4 Your Age

Some say that the older you get, the less affected you are by cannabis. Others believe that the younger you are, the more likely you are to enjoy marijuana. There isn't necessarily a study on the matter, but your age does play a role in your cannabis high.

(Shown Left: Cannabis Can Benefit All Ages. Photo Credits: Shutterstock)

For instance, it's possible that younger people will feel the effects of THC much faster than older people when eating edibles. This is because younger people have a more efficient digestive system, which allows them to break down edibles quickly.

THC gets you high once it's metabolized into your blood, so it's likely that those who are more healthy will become higher much faster.

#5 The Dosage

Dosage plays a role that directly affects your cannabis high. The dose refers to the amount of THC that you're consuming, and it will affect the way you feel.

(Shown Right: Cannabis Dosage Reference.)

If you're eating cannabis edibles, the difference between a 100mg THC cookie and a 1,000mg THC brownie is *significant*. How big is the difference? It's 10x. To put it into perspective, eating one 1,000mg brownie equates to eating 10 100mg THC cookies.

Now, take the effect that you feel from one 100mg THC cookie and amplify it by 10. Depending on your tolerance and mental strength - this amount may be devastating.

Dosage isn't necessarily the amount of the THC - it's how much you take. For example, you buy a package of gummy bears that contain 10 gummies and are infused with 10mg of THC each. Although the dosage is low, it can become large once you eat the entire package in one sitting. In other words, these 10mg gummies are turned into a 100mg THC beast after consuming 10. What would have been a low dose is turned into a potentially psychedelic experience - depending, once again, on your tolerance.

#6 Your Setting

Have you ever smoked cannabis in the mountains? Have you ever smoked cannabis at the beach? How about indoors in a hot and humid club? All of these locations are *settings*, and they play a significant role in your cannabis high.

(Shown left: Paranoia Reference.)

When you consume cannabis in a relaxing setting, it's likely that your high will reflect this. If you use marijuana in a stressful environment, it's likely that you'll become stressed out during the experience. Our emotional responses commonly feed off of our setting, and this occurs in everyday life - whether you're high or not.

#7 Terpene Content

Recently, terpenes have come under close study due to their incredible ability to affect your high. Terpenes are organic compounds that are found in nearly all plants - including cannabis. Terpenes are responsible for the flavors and aromas of each and every marijuana strain.

For example, the terpene that's responsible for the lavender aroma is called linalool. This terpene is also found in cannabis, and it's now known to decrease stress and elevate your mood. The terpene myrcene, which is responsible for the delicious taste of mangos, is found mainly Indica-dominant strains. This is because myrcene produces the couchlock effect that leaves so many feeling unable to move.

Terpenes, such as these, affect your high in a big way. If you indulge in a cannabis strain with a large dose of myrcene, then you'll surely have an early bedtime. If you consume a strain that's loaded with pinene, then you'll become incredibly aware and alert.

It's due to terpenes that it's slowly becoming less common to claim cannabis groups (Indica, Sativa, and Hybrid) are responsible for the high we feel. Instead, a growing trend is to attribute the *way* we feel to that of terpenes.

POP QUIZ

Question #1: The terpene (BLANK), which is responsible for the delicious taste of mangos, is found mainly Indica-dominant strains.

Answer: _____

Question #2: It's possible that (BLANK) people will feel the effects of THC much faster than older people when eating edibles.

Answer: _____

Question #3: Instead of affecting you instantly, edibles take between (BLANK) to take effect.

Answer: _____

Question #4: The stronger strain may only take one drag to leave you feeling (BLANK), whereas the weaker variety may leave you buzzed.

Answer: _____

8 Ways to Counteract a Too-Intense Cannabis High...

At some point, we all get *too* high. It's in these moments that you wish the effects will stop pounding your body and mind like never-ending waves. Fear and anxiety are the most common symptoms when experiencing a too-intense cannabis high. Join us as we discuss 8 ways to counteract a too-intense high and save your day.

#1 Always Carry CBD

The first and foremost tip in counteracting a too-intense cannabis high is by using CBD. Cannabidiol is a non-psychoactive cannabinoid that has been studied extensively to reduce the efficacy of THC.

(Shown Right: CBD Oil.)

THC is a psychoactive cannabinoid that attaches to the receptors in the endocannabinoid system. The endocannabinoid system is comprised of receptors that affect motor skills, memory, emotions, and organ function. Once THC enters your body, it attaches to receptors and consequently blocks neuro-signals. The effects of being high are the consequence of these blocked receptors.

Now, CBD is called an *allosteric modulator*, which means it has the ability to reduce the size or shape of a receptor in the endocannabinoid system. By doing so, THC can't bind to a receptor and block it.

So, if you are feeling too high, then taking CBD *should* reduce the effects. CBD will take effect nearly instantly, depending on the method of intake, and the overwhelming edge of a too-intense cannabis high should be worn down.

The best CBD products to always have on hand are the types that are fast-acting. A CBD vape pen or liquid tincture is potentially your best bet to reduce the intensity of a high - fast.

#2 Relax

We know, relaxing is always easier said than done when experiencing a too-intense cannabis high. When you realize you're too high, you need to stop everything that you're doing. It's at this point that you need to take stock of the situation and try to calm yourself down.

(Shown left: Meditation.)

The first way to relax is to tell yourself that the high *will* fade away. Cannabis highs will last between 1-2 hours when consumed via concentrate or flower but can last anywhere from 6-18-hours when ingested via edibles. You must convince yourself that it'll be over soon, and the best thing to do is relax.

Understand that it's impossible to overdose on cannabis, so if this fear is playing a large role in your discomfort, rest assured that you'll be ok.

Next, you'll want to take steady, deep breaths. If you practice meditation or yoga; this is the perfect moment to remember your training. Slow and steady breathing is known to help people relax during moments of fear, so this should be one of the first steps in reacting to a too-intense cannabis high.

Once you've reduced your anxiety levels and feel a sense of calm, try your best to remain in a positive state. This means that you should not dwell on the psychoactive effects that are currently plaguing you. Instead, focus on positive thoughts in your mind or tangible things in your physical surroundings.

#3 Drink Water or Tea

It's always recommended to stay hydrated, but even more so when you begin to notice you're getting too high. Water won't necessarily dilute the THC in your system, but you will become hydrated and feel better able to withstand the strong effects.

Tea, however, has a better probability of counteracting a too-intense cannabis high because of its therapeutic qualities. Make sure that the tea that you're using does not have caffeine, as this may increase your overall negative experience.

Tea, such as chamomile or lavender are naturally relaxing; so they are perfect choices when seeking to tone down your high.

#4 Exercise

Sometimes, sweating it out might be the best method in counteracting a too-intense cannabis high. Going for a walk, run, or another non-complicated exercise can significantly reduce the effects that you're feeling.

(Shown Right: Exercising Reference.)

When you move your body, you're less prone to focusing on your fear and anxiety. The primary reason why a cannabis experience is too strong is that you're focusing on the effects that you're feeling. By moving your body and getting your heart rate up, you may find that the symptoms of being too high will decrease.

#5 Prevention is Key

The number one way to counteract a too intense cannabis high is to not get to this point in the first place. Prevention is always more effective than reaction, but few of us practice this. You may wonder - how can you prevent getting too high? Know your limit.

When you understand your limit, you'll never overindulge and get too high. Instead, you'll always stop before feeling the negative effects of consuming too much cannabis. This rule may be difficult for those that are new to marijuana, but for most, it's a method that guarantees success.

The best way to know your limit is to experiment slowly. For example, when you take a drag from a joint of a potent strain, wait a few minutes to gauge the effects. If you feel moderately stoned, then it may be best to wait for the effects to subside before continuing. If the effects are too weak, then you can slowly consume more cannabis. By slowly increasing your dose, you can responsibly gauge where your limit is.

#6 Eat Food

When people become stressed out or afraid, the body reacts by demanding food. This response pushes you to seek the comforting refuge that food has to offer. It doesn't mean that you should order a super-sized pizza, but it does mean that a light snack should be in order.

Something that will make you feel good, such as a salad, is a perfect method to counteract the strong effects of THC. Once you feel comforted by the food you eat, you'll be better able to deal with the lingering effects of THC.

(Shown Above: Sharing food with Friends.)

#7 Black Pepper

Although this method has yet to be scientifically proven, black pepper can be used to counteract a too intense cannabis high. By smelling it or chewing the small peppers, you'll reduce the anxiety that's fueling your negative experience.

It's not that black pepper is known to dilute the effects of THC, but rather, to calm you down. Black pepper has been used to treat anxiety disorders, and this is why it can be used when you've got the fear due to too much marijuana.

#8 Treat Yourself to a Bath

When you're too high, it's an excellent idea to turn your bad experience into a spa day. You don't necessarily need to go to an actual spa, but instead - fill up your bathtub. Hopefully, you're stocked up on bath salts that are loaded with magnesium or essential oils that contain lavender.

(Shown Above: Relaxing Bath.)

Don't make the water too hot, as it may make you feel even more discomfort if you've become incredibly sensitive to physical aspects. Make sure the water is lukewarm, and place the bath salts or essential oils into the tub.

Sit down or sprawl out - either way, enjoy the experience. Take tips from the section regarding relaxation and focus on breathing and positive thoughts.

The reason we recommend using bath salts that contain magnesium is that magnesium is a powerful tool for relaxing. It soothes the body and mind and is proven to reduce stress.

#9 Human Stress Response

Remember, the THC is making you feel uncomfortable, but it's your stress response that magnifies it. This is why the majority of these tips are oriented around reducing your anxiety and fear. If you reduce anxiety and fear, your stress is reduced; therefore, you'll be ready to counteract a too intense cannabis high.

POP QUIZ

Question #1: CBD is called an (BLANK), which means it has the ability to reduce the size or shape of a receptor in the endocannabinoid system.

Answer: _____

Question #2: (BLANK) is always more effective than reaction, but few of us practice this.

Answer: _____

Question #3: Although this method has yet to be scientifically proven, (BLANK) can be used to counteract a too intense cannabis high.

Answer: _____

Question #4: Make sure that the tea that you're using does not have (BLANK), as this may increase your overall negative experience.

Answer: _____

Low and Slow: Best Cannabis Strains for Beginners...

Most of us recall the first time that we overindulged in alcohol, and we all remember the hangover. Nobody wants an equally unpleasant first cannabis experience. With the overwhelming number of cannabis strains on the market today, even experienced tokers get confused.

(Shown Above: Cannabis Journal.)

Best Cannabis Strains for Beginners

As mentioned above, beginners should be careful about how much THC they ingest. A good way to go about it is to select cannabis strains with high CBD levels. CBD tends to counteract the psychoactive effects of THC and these strains will give you a soothing effect with minimal psychoactive effects. If you want to use cannabis for recreational purposes, check out some of the milder strains we suggest below.

Harlequin

Harlequin contains a high CBD content with a THC level of between 4-7%. Doctors often suggest this strain for its anti-anxiety and pain-relieving properties.

(Shown Right: Harlequin. Photo Credits: Learn Sativa)

Harlequin suits beginners who want a gradual introduction to the psychoactive effects of THC. Sativa-dominant Harlequin provides users with the therapeutic properties of CBD without leaving them feeling overly sedated. The sweet, fruity flavors are perfect for beginners who might not be ready to appreciate more earthy cannabis strains. You may want to try other high-CBD strains, such as Cannatonic and ACDC.

Hindu Kush

A pure indica strain, Hindu Kush imparts dreamy, relaxing feelings. Patients often choose Kush varieties for insomnia and pain relief.

(Shown Left: Hindu Kush. Photo Credits: WeedAdvisor)

Kush has a mood-lifting, yet sedative effect which makes it an excellent choice for when you're sick in bed or want to spend a relaxing Sunday afternoon watching movies. Kush strains tend to fall between 15-20% THC, which will not be overwhelming for beginners. The many strains of Kush have a wide spectrum of flavor profiles from earthy and spicy to sweet and fruity.

White Widow

If you're the kind of person who falls asleep in yoga class, you might want to try White Widow for a more balanced indica-dominant buzz.

(Shown Right: White Widow. Photo Credits: RedeCan)

White Widow gets its name from the abundance of pearly-white trichomes that dust the surface of the buds. Green House Seed Company unleashed White Widow onto the market in the Netherlands where the strain won first place in the 1995 High Times Cannabis Cup.

Over two decades later, White Widow remains one of the most popular cannabis strains. White Widow strains tend to vary between 20-25% THC. Check the labels, and choose a lower-THC variety if you're not quite ready to try a higher THC strain. With its fresh, subtle flavor, White Widow is an excellent, all-purpose cannabis strain.

Jack Herer

If you're looking for an attitude-adjustment while still getting work done, try Jack Herer. Author of the legendary book, *The Emperor Wears No Clothes*, cannabis activist Jack Herer spent decades tirelessly working to end cannabis prohibition in the United States.

(Shown Right: Jack Herer. Photo Credits: Trippy Cat)

A true cannabis hero, Jack Herer, brought hope to legions of cannabis-connoisseurs. Likewise, his namesake strain lifts the spirits and helps with depression. The slightly earthy and pine-scented flavors provide a nice contrast to some of the sweeter cannabis strains.

Maui Wowie

Are you planning a surfing or hiking trip? Maui Wowie will put you in the perfect head-space to enjoy outdoor activities. Because Maui Wowie strains usually stay under 20% THC, you'll have plenty of energy with just enough psychedelic effects to get you in the groove.

(Shown Left: Mowie Wowie. Photo Credits: Stoner Things)

This tropical blend helps with aches and pains, including migraines. Medicinal marijuana doctors often prescribe Maui Wowie for cancer patients to fight nausea and improve appetite. True Maui Wowie imparts a sweet aroma and flavor with hints of pineapple and citrus. Make sure you buy a batch that has been cultivated in Hawaii. The volcanic soil makes a difference in capturing the unique fruitiness of a Maui Wowie strain.

POP QUIZ

Question #1: Medicinal marijuana doctors often prescribe (BLANK) for cancer patients to fight nausea and improve appetite.

Answer: _____

Question #2: (BLANK). Author of the legendary book, *The Emperor Wears No Clothes*.

Answer: _____

Question #3: (BLANK) strains tend to vary between 20-25% THC.

Answer: _____

Question #4: (BLANK) has a mood-lifting, yet sedative effect which makes it an excellent choice for when you're sick in bed or want to spend a relaxing Sunday afternoon watching movies.

Answer: _____

Microdosing With Cannabis:
Benefits *without the Buzz...*

Cannabis legalization has created an entirely new group of users: microdosers. These individuals seek the benefits of THC without psychoactive effects. The reason? So they can continue to function during their daily lives without being impaired by THC. Read along to discover the benefits of THC *without* the buzz.

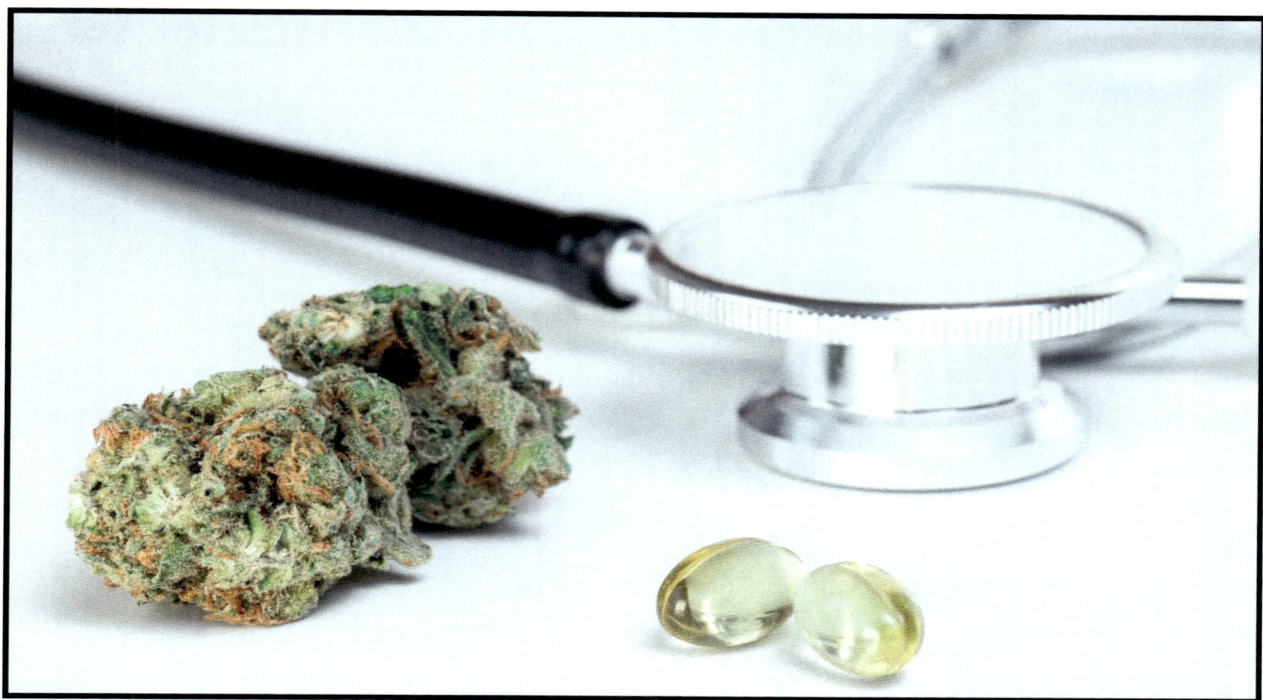

(Shown Above: Cannabis as Medicine.)

The Psychoactive Effects of THC

Tetrahydrocannabinol, also known as THC, is the psychoactive component of marijuana. When smoked, eaten, or vaporized, the THC activates and impairs various receptors in your brain. These receptors are known as the CB1 and CB2 receptor groups, which are part of the endocannabinoid system.

The CB1 and CB2 receptor groups are responsible for a wide host of effects within your body, such as your immune system and various organs. When you experience the sensation of getting high, it's due to THC blocking the CB1 receptors from performing their job.

One of the primary functions of the CB1 receptor group is memory, motor skills, and emotional responses. As you consume large doses of THC, you further block these responses - which translates into a stronger high.

Why Microdose?

If you've never micro-dosed before, then this is probably the first question that comes to mind. There's a multitude of reasons why you'd take small doses of THC products instead of a single, large dose.

Overall, micro-dosing allows you to help relieve various issues while remaining in control of your life. If you consume too much THC, then you aren't entirely in control of your actions.

When it comes to cannabis and THC, there's a fine line, and if you cross it, you'll become *too* high. When you want to enjoy the benefits that THC has to offer, then you'll want to stay behind this invisible line. To do this, it takes experience. Each of our bodies is different, and it's likely that we all have different tolerances to various amounts of THC.

You might still wonder: why go through so much work to find this fine line? Let's take a look at how microdosing can benefit you in your day-to-day life.

#1 Function at Work

As you already know, large doses of cannabis will make you incredibly high. In a work environment, this is possibly one of the worst things you can do. However, many of you use cannabis for a variety of reasons, such as relieving stress, anxiety, anti-social tendencies, and pain.

So, how can you use marijuana at work to reduce various symptoms without becoming too high? The answer is simple: microdose. By lowering your dosage, you'll feel the benefits of THC without becoming too high to perform your job.

If you require the benefits that THC has to offer, then you'll want to keep a low dosage to prevent yourself from being reprimanded by your boss in the event that you get too high. Overall, micro-dosing will help you stay focused on the tasks at hand, all while remaining functional.

#2 Study Harder and with More Focus

Countless college students use cannabis to study due to THC's ability to heighten your awareness, motivation, and focus. These three traits are perfect for studying, but if you indulge too much, these beneficial traits will become overwhelming and destroy your drive to study.

By micro-dosing, you'll remain capable of paying attention to the task at hand, without drifting into tangents. If you become too high, then it's likely that you won't be able to focus efficiently; thus, your study session will suffer.

#3 Enjoy Social Interactions

Many of us suffer from social anxiety, and THC helps by reducing the barrier for social interactions. When you microdose THC, you can fine-tune your overall experience. If you find that you can reduce the "edge" of social interactions, you can slightly increase your next dose to reach the perfect level.

If you blow past the point of no return, then it's likely that you'll be too high to carry on a normal conversation. Additionally, you may increase your social anxiety, thus making it far worse.

#4 Find Relief for Some Chronic Conditions

Millions of Americans suffer from chronic conditions, such as MS, Alzheimer's, arthritis, cancer, COPD, Crohn's Disease, and many more. Cannabis has been studied to help relieve symptoms from chronic conditions, but it's far more effective at smaller doses to extend the relief. Instead of consuming a massive dose of THC, you'll be able to decrease symptoms while remaining cognitive.

#5 Assist with Mental Disorders

Just like chronic conditions, millions of Americans suffer from mental disorders. This category includes PTSD, depression, anxiety, eating disorders, OCD, schizophrenia, bipolar disorder, phobias, addictions, and ADD.

By micro-dosing, users can keep symptoms in check without significantly increasing their tolerance. If you consume a hefty dose of THC all at once, you'll quickly boost your tolerance to THC - which makes it less effective. Increasing your tolerance when you're using THC as a medicine is the last thing you want to do.

How To Microdose...

Micro-dosing isn't as hard as you might think. As long as you have a bit of patience, you'll find the proper dose to effectively microdose - every time.

First, you'll need to start *slowly*. If you're smoking cannabis, then you should use a small joint or pipe. Start with one small puff and wait 10-15 minutes to gauge your overall feelings. If you aren't feeling any relief, then you can take another small hit. Continue bumping up your dose until you feel relief, but without being *too* high.

You'll find that one drag too long will result in too much THC, so everything needs to be done in micro amounts. While you're experimenting, it's crucial that you take note as to how much you're taking, which strain, and method. You need to take notes so you can replicate this experience over and over after you've found the right amount.

This can be applied when using any device or method to consume cannabis. Vaporizers, edibles, and concentrates can all be fine-tuned to find the perfect dose.

Edibles are more tricky to microdose compared to all other methods because they take a significant amount of time to take effect. This is because the THC needs to pass through your digestive system and into your blood. Once this happens, you'll feel the psychoactive effects of THC. The process of digestion can take anywhere from 2-4 hours, which is a substantial amount of time to wait.

When attempting to microdose with edibles, you should take half the recommended dose. Your patience will eventually pay off, and you'll be able to take edibles anytime and anywhere. This ability will free you to use edibles anywhere you please, which is beneficial for those who can no longer smoke cannabis.

Which Method is Best For Microdosing?

This question will generate multiple answers - depending on who you're talking to. Each method for micro-dosing poses pros and cons, so let's take a look at each.

A. Vaping

Vaping THC is an excellent way to microdose because it's discreet, portable, and contains a measured dose. You can take small or large hits easily, which further increases the ability of vaporizers to provide accurate doses.

The only downside that could be associated with using a vaporizer for micro-dosing is its' cost. However, vaporizers have become immensely popular amongst cannabis enthusiasts; thus, their prices have come down.

B. Edibles

As mentioned previously, edibles are the trickiest cannabis product to microdose with. This is due to the time it takes for a marijuana-infused edible to find its way into your blood via digestion.

Most edibles are labeled with their total amount of THC, but each person will react differently to the same dose. However, edibles are in high demand because they're discreet and don't require you to smoke.

Once you've found the sweet spot with edibles, you can efficiently microdose virtually anywhere. These cannabis-infused foods don't smell like marijuana, and they're usually in the guise of baked goods or harmless-looking sweets.

On the other hand, edibles can frustrate individuals with long wait times and improper doses. Additionally, once you find an edible that works - you'll likely need to stay with it.

C. Smoking

The smoking category incorporates pipes, bongs, joints, and blunts. Each of these methods is suitable for micro-dosing, except bongs. Unless your tolerance is sky-high, there's no real reason why you would use a bong to achieve a microdose of THC.

A single drag from a joint or pipe should be sufficient, depending on your current tolerance levels. The only downside of micro-dosing with these methods is that a pipe or joint will exude a pungent aroma of burned marijuana long after it's been put out.

D. **Dabbing**

Dabbing is incredibly popular amongst cannabis enthusiasts but isn't suitable for those who are new to this revolutionary product. When you dab, you smoke *high* concentrations of THC extract. These can range upwards of 99% THC, which is far too potent for those seeking to *micro*dose. Unless your tolerance is outrageously high, it's unlikely that this method is suitable.

An Ever-Changing Tolerance

As you continually consume cannabis, your tolerance to THC will eventually increase. This means that your perfect dose will soon become obsolete. Once this occurs, you'll be required to begin the entire process of micro-dosing all over again.

This is an aspect that none of us can escape, and depending on how much THC you're consuming, the time it takes will be shorter or longer. If you take a single puff once a day, your overall tolerance to THC won't change nearly as fast as someone who takes 10 puffs in a single day. As you can see, your tolerance is solely affected by your daily THC intake.

As long as you keep track of the dose that you repeat, you can slowly increase it if you find that your microdose is too *micro*. With a bit of experimentation, you'll be back to your perfect THC level.

How Microdosing Can <u>Change</u> Cannabis Culture

Up until this point, the vast majority of cannabis enthusiasts have sought THC for recreational use. Legalization (recreational or medicinal) opened the door to an entirely new crowd that wasn't willing to use marijuana during prohibition.

This new crowd demands functionality in their daily lives, but enjoy the beneficial effects of THC. As thousands of new users try cannabis, the entire idea of cannabis culture is changing before our eyes.

Although there are those who wish to get as stoned as humanly possible, there's a rising trend to be *functionally high*. This new group is quickly normalizing cannabis use because it doesn't advocate becoming too stoned. Instead, it presents marijuana as a supplement, rather than a drug. Just how millions of individuals wake up each morning and demand coffee, so are those who microdose cannabis.

Cannabis contains a plethora of benefits that can help countless individuals with their day-to-day life. Medical patients, students, and business people can all microdose THC to their benefit.

POP QUIZ

Question #1: As you continually consume cannabis, your tolerance to THC will eventually (BLANK).

Answer: _____

Question #2: The smoking category incorporates pipes, bongs, joints, and blunts. Each of these methods is suitable for micro-dosing, except (BLANK).

Answer: _____

Question #3: (BLANK) are more tricky to microdose compared to all other methods because they take a significant amount of time to take effect.

Answer: _____

Question #4: (BLANK) allows you to help relieve various issues while remaining in control of your life. If you consume too much THC, then you aren't entirely in control of your actions.

Answer: _____

PAGE 16 - POP QUIZ ANSWERS

Question #1: What's the highest paying career in the cannabis industry? (**ANSWER:** Dispensary Manager)

Question #2: Who is responsible for overseeing the production of cannabis concentrates, the safety of your workers, and the protocols put in place? (**ANSWER:** Extraction Leader)

Question #3: This job entails the management of thousands of plants that are at different stages of life. Seedlings, clones, vegetative stage, flowering phase; along with the subsequent harvest and post-harvest process. (**ANSWER:** Master Grower)

PAGE 26 - POP QUIZ ANSWERS

Question #1: Hybrids contain a mixture of indica and sativa effects.

Question #2: Hybridization occurs *when the mother is an indica, and the father is a sativa - or vice versa.*

Question #3: Name 5 popular indica strains.
- Master Kush
- Bubba Kush
- Granddaddy Purple
- Blackberry Kush
- Hindu Kush
- G13
- Hash Plant
- Herijuana
- Black Domina
- Blueberry

PAGE 37 - POP QUIZ ANSWERS

Question #1: Ruderalis is a small group that produces autoflowering genetics.

Question #2: United States passed the Farm Bill in 2018, which allows farmers to cultivate hemp - as long as it contained less than 0.3% THC.

Question #3: Alternatively, it was found that hemp cultivars contained far more CBD.

PAGE 57 - POP QUIZ ANSWERS

Question #1: (BLANK) was the first endocannabinoid to be discovered. This molecule is a partial activator (agonist) for both CB1 and CB2 receptors.
(**ANSWER:** Anandamide)

Question #2: These are the small molecules that activate the cannabinoid receptors…
(**ANSWER:** Endocannabinoids)

Question #3: When it comes to cannabis flowers, the overall quality of the weed will be determined during the growth, harvest, and (BLANK) process. (**ANSWER:** Curing)

PAGE 68 - POP QUIZ ANSWERS

Question #1: For example, (BLANK), a scent of terpene-soaking pine, works well with THC and reduces the weed-degrading effect of memory. (**ANSWER:** Alpha Pine)

Question #2: (BLANK) is now the focus of such effects and goes to show it's incredible power to relax your body and mind. (**ANSWER:** Myrcene)

Question #3: Cannabis contains over how many different molecules called cannabinoids? (**ANSWER:** 100+)

PAGE 78 - POP QUIZ ANSWERS

Question #1: This means that the higher the terpene concentration, the more effective your cannabis strain will be in delivering medicinal or therapeutic qualities.

Question #2: Most marijuana strains contain between 14-22% THC, with incredibly potent varieties ranging between 23-35% THC.

Question #3: CBD is the second most common cannabinoid that's found in cannabis, and the most common cannabinoid found in industrial hemp.

PAGE 96 - POP QUIZ ANSWERS

Question #1: (Delta 9 THC) is probably the best-known cannabinoid.

Question #2: The most significant difference between cannabis-infused food and dried flowers is the *absorption rate*.

Question #3: On average, most users that experience cannabis edibles are high from 3-8 hours - with some extended effects lasting an eye-popping 16 hours.

Question #4: CBN is the strongest cannabinoid that has been identified to promote sleep, making CBN-rich cannabis an ideal treatment for insomnia.

Question #5: CBGA appears to act as a weak affinity antagonist for the body's CB1 receptor, making the body more susceptible to cannabinoids in cannabis.

PAGE 102 - POP QUIZ ANSWERS

Question #1: A popular solvent to extract cannabinoids is butane.

Question #2: This method is called decarboxylation, and it's the reaction that's responsible for THC becoming psychoactive.

Question #3: Where cannabis flowers may have upwards of a 1-2% terpene concentration, marijuana extracts can have 8-10%.

PAGE 110 - POP QUIZ ANSWERS

Question #1: Topical treatments won't make you high, even if they contain THC.

Question #2: Vaping is not considered a 'smoking' method, but rather an 'inhalation' method.

Question #3: If you have a lung condition, for example, you wouldn't opt for smoking.

Question #4: Some people claim that raw cannabis juice has calming and pain-fighting effects, but so far, no scientific research has been conducted on it.

Question #5: The cannabinoids absorb into the capillaries in your mouth.

PAGE 116 - POP QUIZ ANSWERS

Question #1: The terpene myrcene, which is responsible for the delicious taste of mangos, is found mainly Indica-dominant strains.

Question #2: It's possible that younger people will feel the effects of THC much faster than older people when eating edibles.

Question #3: Instead of affecting you instantly, edibles take between 1-3 hours to take effect.

Question #4: The stronger strain may only take one drag to leave you feeling dazed, whereas the weaker variety may leave you buzzed.

PAGE 122 - POP QUIZ ANSWERS

Question #1: CBD is called an *allosteric modulator*, which means it has the ability to reduce the size or shape of a receptor in the endocannabinoid system.

Question #2: Prevention is always more effective than reaction, but few of us practice this.

Question #3: Although this method has yet to be scientifically proven, black pepper can be used to counteract a too intense cannabis high.

Question #4: Make sure that the tea that you're using does not have caffeine, as this may increase your overall negative experience.

PAGE 128 - POP QUIZ ANSWERS

Question #1: Medicinal marijuana doctors often prescribe Maui Wowie for cancer patients to fight nausea and improve appetite.

Question #2: Jack Herer. Author of the legendary book, *The Emperor Wears No Clothes*.

Question #3: White Widow strains tend to vary between 20-25% THC.

Question #4: Kush has a mood-lifting, yet sedative effect which makes it an excellent choice for when you're sick in bed or want to spend a relaxing Sunday afternoon watching movies.

PAGE 137 - POP QUIZ ANSWERS

Question #1: As you continually consume cannabis, your tolerance to THC will eventually increase.

Question #2: The smoking category incorporates pipes, bongs, joints, and blunts. Each of these methods is suitable for micro-dosing, except bongs.

Question #3: Edibles are more tricky to microdose compared to all other methods because they take a significant amount of time to take effect.

Question #4: Micro-dosing allows you to help relieve various issues while remaining in control of your life. If you consume too much THC, then you aren't entirely in control of your actions.

How to Grow Cannabis (Step-by-Step)

As you move through the plants life stages, it's important to remember that each phase requires different care towards the plant. Simply keep an eye on the **Environmental Checklist** *for each phase and your plant will do just fine.*

1. Germination/Propagation *(Page 157)*
2. Seedling *(Page 159)*
3. Vegetative *(Page 165)*
4. Flower *(Page 169)*

(Followed by Harvesting, Drying and Curing your cannabis.) *(Pages 171 & 173)*

During each stage or phase I challenge you to focus on the **7 key elements** *to your garden. We place these on your* **Environmental Checklist** *for each life stage of your plant to make things easier to manage.*

1. Light Schedule
2. PPFD *(Page 148)*
3. Spectrum
4. Temperature *(Page 153)*
5. Humidity *(Page 153)*
6. Soil Moisture & PH *(Page 154)*
7. Water PH *(Page 155)*

IMPORTANT : Pay close attention as we show you how to measure each of the 7 key elements on your **Environmental Checklist**.

How to Test Your PPFD

Instead of paying upwords $150-$550 for a PAR/ Quantum meter that reads LED. Simply purchase a LUX meter like the one below for $20 and use our LUX to PAR calculator: https://learnsativa.org/lux-to-par-calculator/ *(As shown on next page)*

PAR is photosynthetic active radiation. **PAR light** is the wavelengths of **light** within the visible range of 400 to 700 nanometers (nm) which drive photosynthesis (Figure 1). **PAR** is a much used (and often misused) term related to horticulture **lighting**. **PAR** is NOT a measurement or "metric" like feet, inches or kilos.

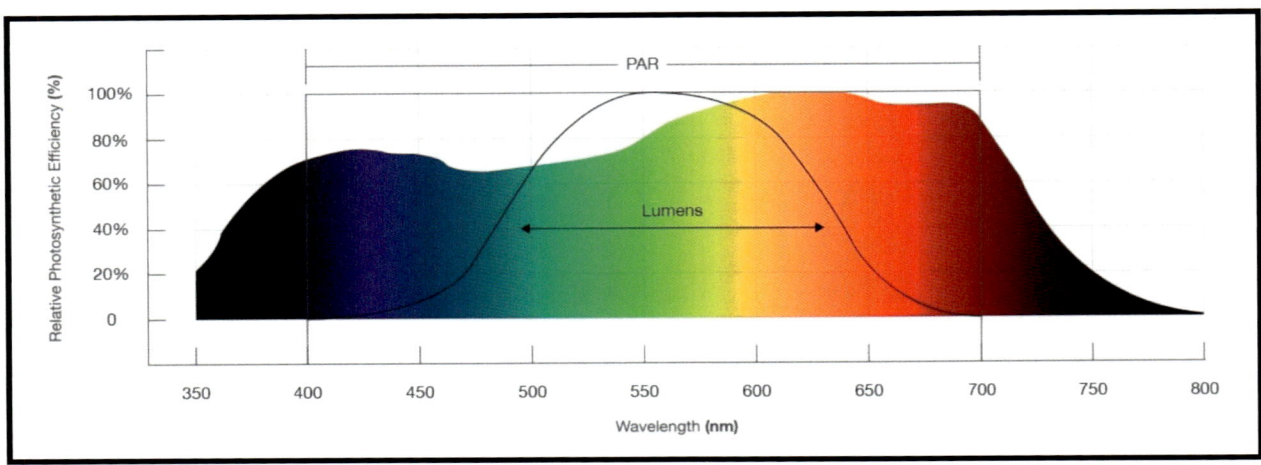

(Shown Above: Figure 1. Photo & PAR Definition Credits: Fluence)

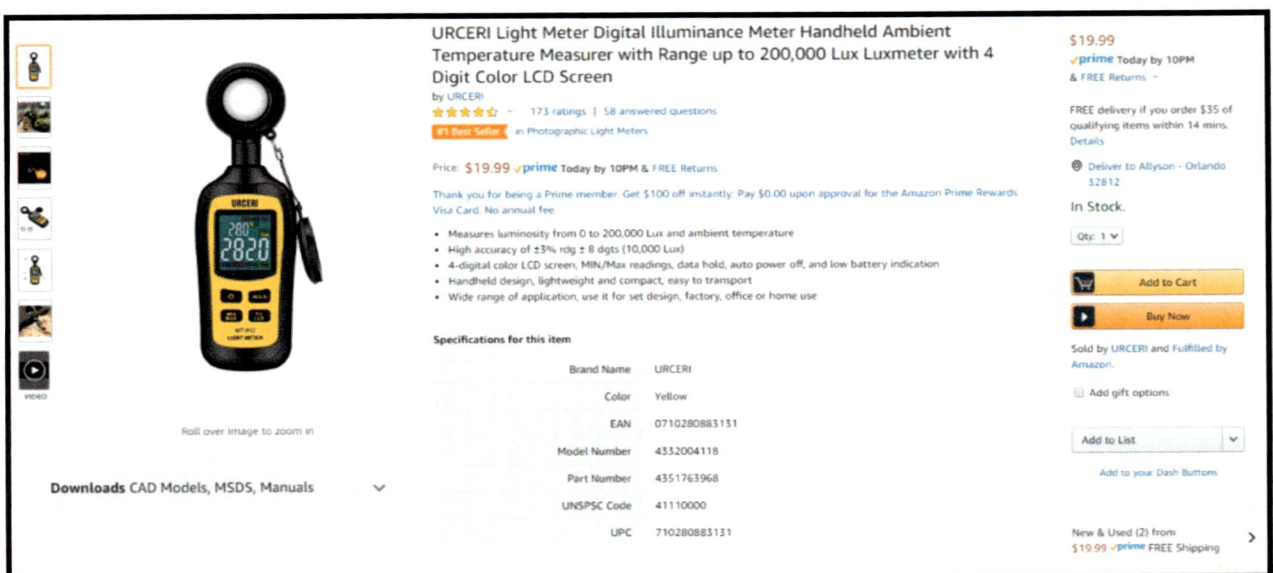

(Shown Above: URCERI Lux Meter. Photo Credits: Amazon)

When using Learn Sativa's LUX to PAR calculator, be sure to check your lights spectrum. Typically manufacturers will provide you with this information when purchasing from a reputable company.

Note: Most PH meters require you to calibrate the device using powders provided in the package - read the directions provided by the manufacturer and calibrate regularly.

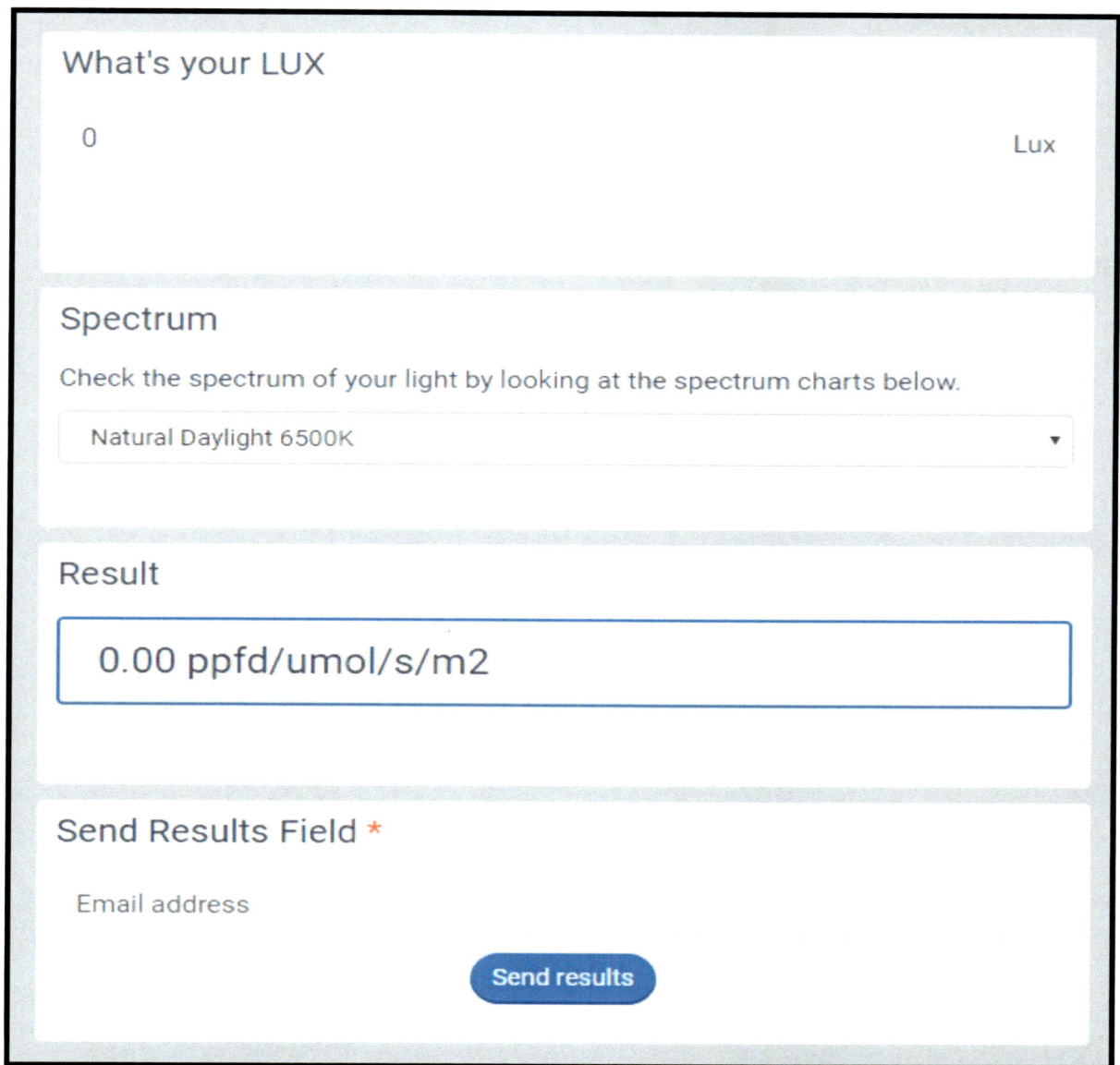

(Shown Above: LUX to PAR Calculator. Photo Credits: LearnSativa.org)

Where do I put my PAR Meter Sensor?

Let's say the image below is your typical 4' x 4' garden.

We always want to get the highest PPFD reading needed in the center of our light because the more we move away from the center of the light the less powerful the light will be in regards to PPFD readings.

Example: Vegetative Requires 400-600 PPFD in order for the plants to thrive. Therefore, I would want to take the high side of this reading (600) from the CENTER of my light (*See the yellow crosshair on the garden image below*). That way as I move the sensor of my PAR meter away from the center of my light I can find out where my low end (400) is and that would give me my lights optimal vegetative coverage capability. (See image below)

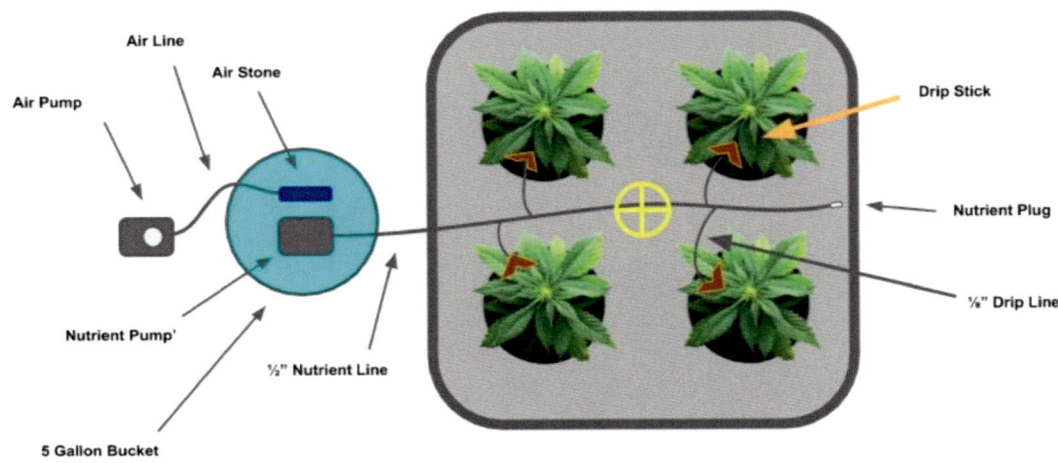

(Shown Above: 4' x 4' Garden Illustration Photo Credits: LearnSativa.org)

What is Canopy Height?

Canopy Height Measurements are the distance from the bottom of your light to the top of your plants.

You control the PPFD of a light simply by changing the distance the meter is from the light. *The closer you put the sensor to the light, the **higher your PPFD** reading would be. The further you move the sensor away from the light source, the **lower your PPFD** reading would be.*

HLG 65...
Suggested Height for Veg 12-15"
Actual Height We Used > 11.5"

(Shown Above: Canopy Height Illustration. Photo Credits: LearnSativa.org)

PPFD Chart Example

The image below was a PPFD reading we took on the HLG 65 LED grow light. Notice how the PPFD reading is much more powerful in the center and then begins to drop as the readings are taken further away from the center of the light.

Based on this lights PPFD readings, the only usable canopy coverage is 1' x 1'.

HLG 65 PPFD

In order for our plants to thrive during the vegetative stage, it's recommended we stay within 400-600 PPFD.

All PAR readings were taken by:
Apogee Quantum Meters

Each Box Represents 6sq Inches*

125	242	255	144
233	515	517	254
237	494	479	228
115	212	193	120

⬤ Center tested at **630**

(Shown Above: HLG 65 LED PPFD Readings. Photo Credits: LearnSativa.org)

How to Test Your Humidity and Temperature

Testing your humidity and temperature are vital to your plants overall health. Amazon has pretty affordable Hygrometers and Thermometers for sale. The one below is a personal favorite, however the screen tends to fog up if placed inside a humidity dome.

Simply set this device inside your tent and monitor the humidity on the top (both high & low) along with the tents temperature (high & low).

Try your best to keep this monitor as close to the plants as possible.

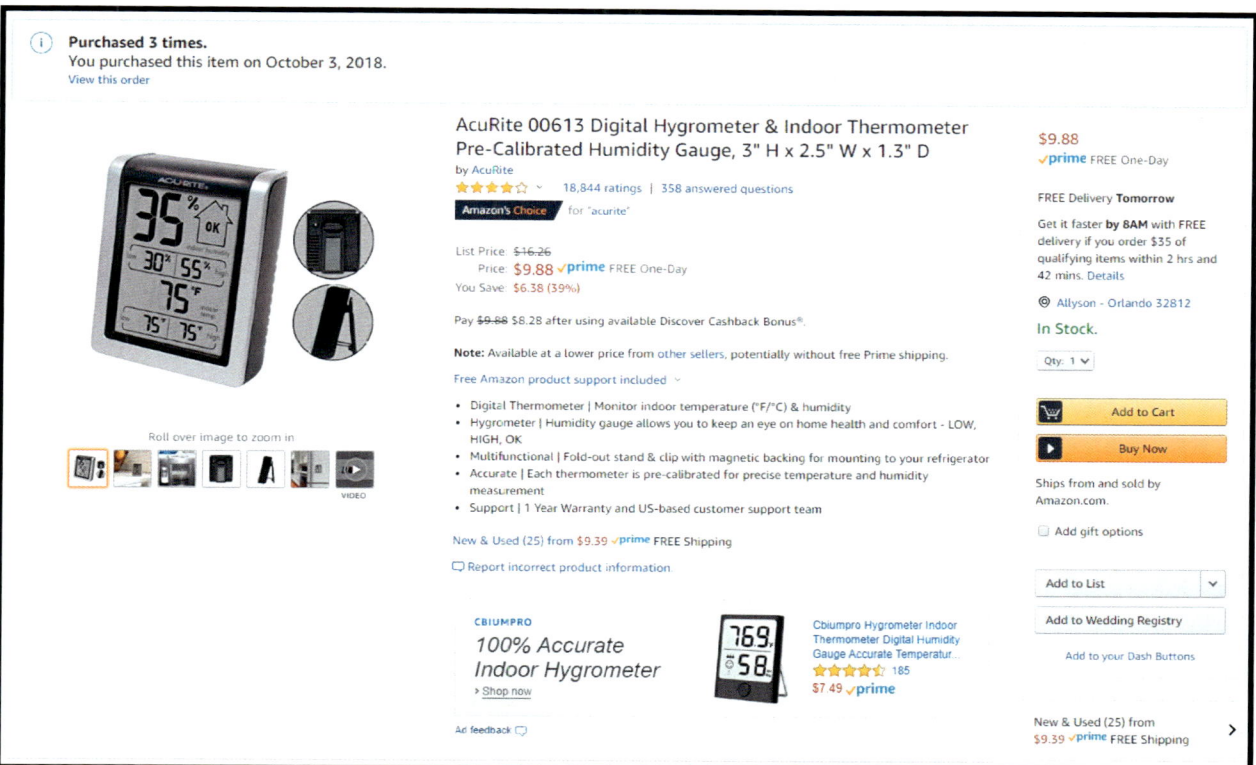

(Shown Above: AcuRite Digital Hygrometer and Thermometer. Photo Credits: Amazon)

How to Test Your Soils Moisture & PH

Over watering your plants can lead to mold, mildew and a number of other problems. We suggest buying a soil meter and testing your soil on the regular. Most meters have 3 readings "Dry, Moist, Wet". We're looking for more of a moist reading in our garden.

Remember: Cannabis is NOT grass - water your plants when the lights first come on.

(Shown Above: 3 in 1 Soil Moisture Meter. Photo Credits: Amazon)

How to Test Your Water PH

Using a PH meter is as simple as pulling off the cap to the device and sticking it in the water you wish to test. Your PH reading will be displayed on the LED screen within seconds.

Note: Most PH meters require you to calibrate the device using powders provided in the package - read the directions provided by the manufacturer and calibrate regularly.

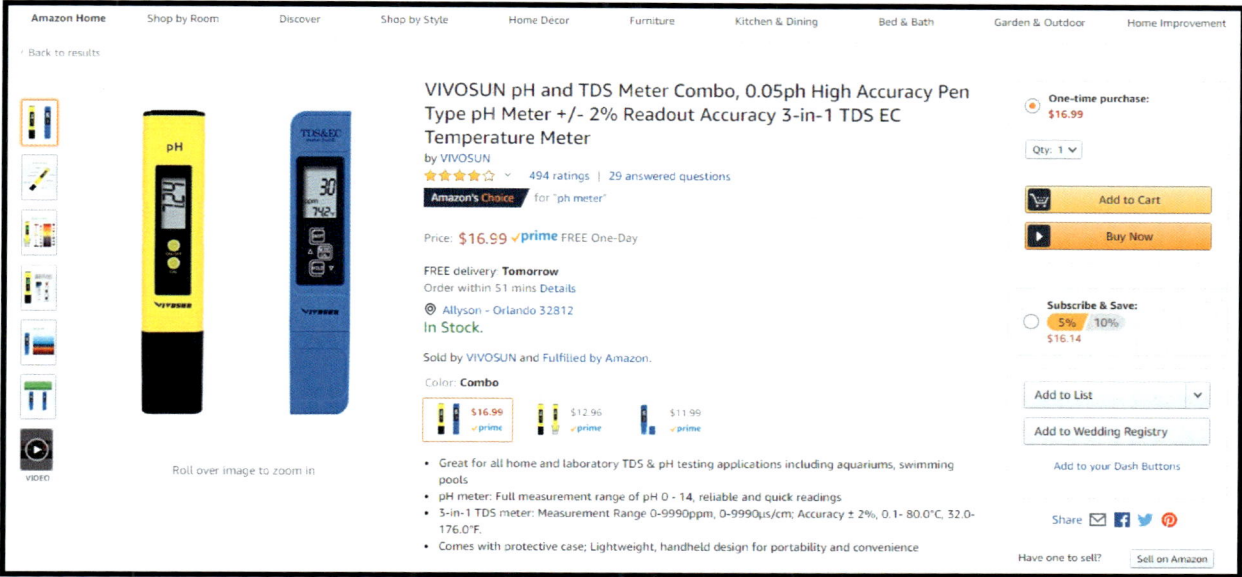

(Shown Above: PC & TDS meter Combo. Photo Credits: Amazon)

Production Schedule (Overview)

This **production schedule** will give you a better idea of what's to come with your next grow. Each week and phase of the plants life will require different lighting, nutrients, and pruning techniques. Lucky for you, we have to put together everything you need to know in order to get your grow thriving in no time.

REMINDER: Be sure to review your **environmental checklist** for each stage of the plants life cycle, this will give you a better idea of what tasks will be required of you.

Propagation/Germination/Seedling (2 Week Cycle) *(Page 157)*
Week One
Week Two: Setup Grow Tent *(Page 161)*

Vegetative Phase (6 Week Cycle) *(Page 165)*
Week Three: Transplant
Week Four: Top/Fim plant
Week Five (Prune)
Week Six: Top/Fim plant
Week Seven (Prune)
Week Eight: Top/Fim plant

Flower Phase (8 Week Cycle) *(Page 169)*
Week Eleven: Transplant & Scrog
Week Twelve (Prune)
Week Three (Final Prune)
Week Four
Week Five
Week Six
Week Seven
Week Eight

Harvest *(Page 170)*

Drying Guide (1 Week Cycle) *(Page 171)*

Cure Guide (3-4 Week Cycle) *(Page 173)*

Germination Phase

During this phase, you must keep your environment and tools as sterile as possible. The last thing you want to do is cross contaminate or invite disease into your garden. You may not see anything wrong with your plants now, but you can set yourself up for failure come Flower Phase by not taking care of your plants in the Seedling Phase.

The one thing we can't buy back is time - so don't waste it!

Here is what you will need:

1. Seeds
2. Drinking Glass or Mason Jar
3. PH Balanced Water (6.5) Room Temp
4. Paper Towel
5. Large Ceramic Plate

(Shown Above: Parts List. Photo Credits: LearnSativa.org)

Germination Phase Instructions:

1. Fill glass jar with PH balanced water at **room temperature**.
2. Place seeds in PH balanced water (Notice how the seeds **float on top** of the water…)
3. Place glass jar in a dark place, preferably room temperature place.
   NOTE: Kitchen cabinets are a great place to store mason jar while germinating.
4. **Every 2 hours** for 18 hours - **Tap seeds** to the point of submersion. **Goal:** Get seeds to sink to bottom of mason jar.
   NOTE: It's ok if some of the seeds do not sink to the bottom.
5. Place sheet of paper towel on large ceramic plate
6. **Carefully** pour glass jar contents directly onto paper towel.
7. **Spread out** seeds on paper towel.
8. **Carefully** fold the paper towel over.
9. **Place in dark,** humid place (3-4 days)
   NOTE: Kitchen cabinets are a great place to store plate/napkin while germinating
10. Keep paper towel moist, **but not soaked.**
    NOTE: Use a spray bottle with PH balanced water to keep paper towel moist.
11. Periodically unfold your paper towel and check for signs of the "Taproot".
    NOTE: We are looking for a ¼" tap root or "tail" on the seed.
12. Place seedling ½" deep in 8oz soil pot **(tap root facing down!)**
    NOTE: We prefer **Fox Farm Ocean Forest** soil.
13. Place 8oz soil pot in Propagation Dome
14. Continue to **Seedling Phase** procedures.

(Shown Above: Key Germination Points Illustration. Photo Credits: LearnSativa.org)

Seedling Phase

You will be preparing your seedlings for transplanting during this phase. It is important no to shock or overwhelm your plant by stressing it out. You can easily have your female plants turn into males if you don't care for them properly. We call these plants "hermies".

Here is what you will need:

1. T5 Lighting System
2. Humidity Dome Kit
3. Seedling Heating Pad
4. Humidity/ Temperature Reader
5. Soil Moisture Reader
6. Water Bottle with PH (6.5) Room Temp Water
7. Watering Bucket

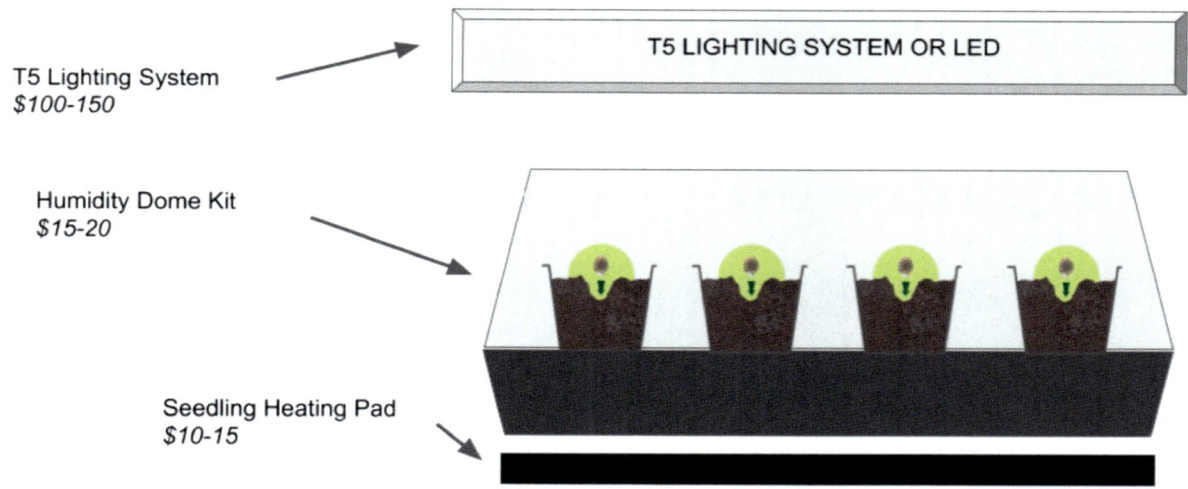

T5 Lighting System
$100-150

Humidity Dome Kit
$15-20

Seedling Heating Pad
$10-15

(Shown Above: Ideal Seedling Environment. Photo Credits: LearnSativa.org)

Seedling Environmental Conditions Checklist

1. **LIGHTS ON: 18 Hours**
   Example: 7:00am - 1:00am

2. **LIGHTS OFF: 6 Hours**
   Example: 1:00am - 7:00am

3. **PPFD:** 200-300

4. **SPECTRUM:** Blue (6500k)

5. **TEMP:** 68-77°F (20-25°C)

6. **HUMIDITY:** 70%

7. **SOIL AND WATER PH:** 6.5

(Shown Above & Right: Seedling Growth.)

Tent Setup List

*The following is just a list of equipment we'd recommend for your Caregiver Grow. You can switch up the size of your tent if you like, just stick to the **Environmental Checklist** and ensure you vegatate your plants within the confines of your tent size. The last thing you want to do is have a plant that's too tall for your tent.*

1. 4' x 4' x 8' tall Grow Tent
2. One Circulating Fan
3. One Charcoal Filter
4. One Inline Grow Fan
5. A full spectrum LED light capable of providing your plants 4' x 4' canopy between 400 -1,000 PPFD (Minimum Requirements)

IMPORTANT: Your LED light is probably the most important investment you'll make aside from your seeds. You can watch more about LED lighting and how to pick the **RIGHT LIGHT** for your grow by scanning the interactive QR code to the right.

The **Under $400** Grow Tent System

Vented Grow Tent Setup

Top View of 4x4 Tent (w/o Plants)

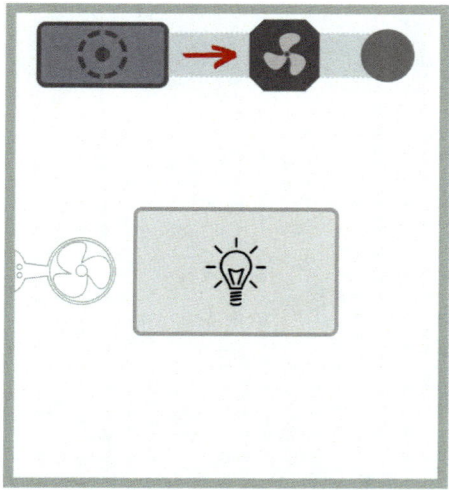

Side View of 4x4 Tent

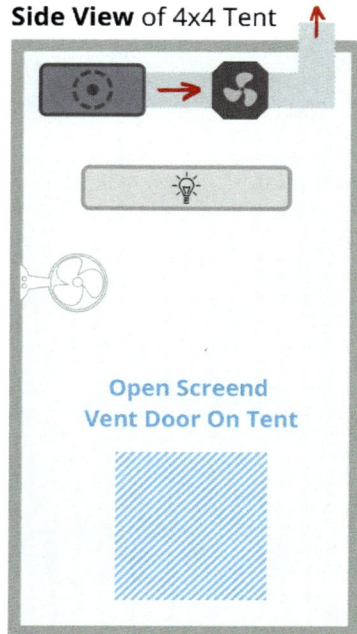

Cool Air will enter the screened vent door at the bottom of the tent while the **Hot Air** will be removed through the top of the tent using the 4" fan and filter combo

ProTip: LED's will reduce the cost of venting dramatically, however be aware of cheap knock-offs.

(Shown Above: Key Germination Points Illustration. Photo Credits: LearnSativa.org)

Drip Fed Irrigation System Parts List

Drip fed irrigation systems are great for a number of reasons. They have the ability to automate your entire watering schedule and scale from as little as 1 plant to 1,000's of plants once you understand the components and theory as to how the system works.

6. **Nutrient Pump (Water Pump)** *$10-15*
7. **Air Pump** *$10-15*
8. **Air Stone** *$2*
9. **Air Line** *$10 a roll*
10. **½" Nutrient Line** *$10-20 a roll*
11. **⅛" Drip Line** *$10 a roll*
12. **Drip Sticks aka "Dripper Stake"** *$1-2 each*
13. **½" Nutrient Line Plug** *$0.80*
14. **Digital Timer** *$15-20*
15. **Surge Protector** *$10-15*
16. **Flood Table** *$150-200*
17. **½" PVC Pipe and Elbows** *$20-30 total*
18. **5 Gallon Bucket** *$5*

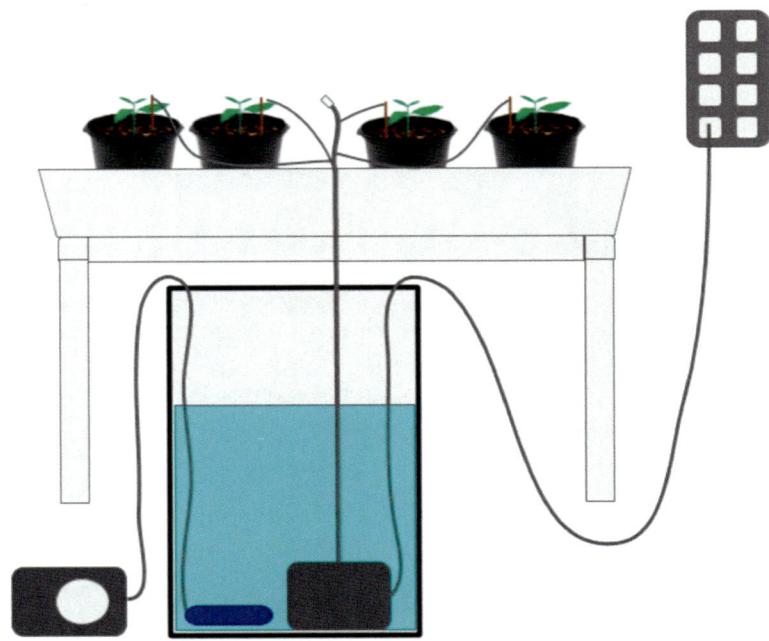

(Shown Above: Drip Fed Irrigation System Illustration. Photo Credits: LearnSativa.org)

Drip Fed Irrigation System (Parts List View)

IMPORTANT: *Keep all electrical devices and plugs above waist level.*

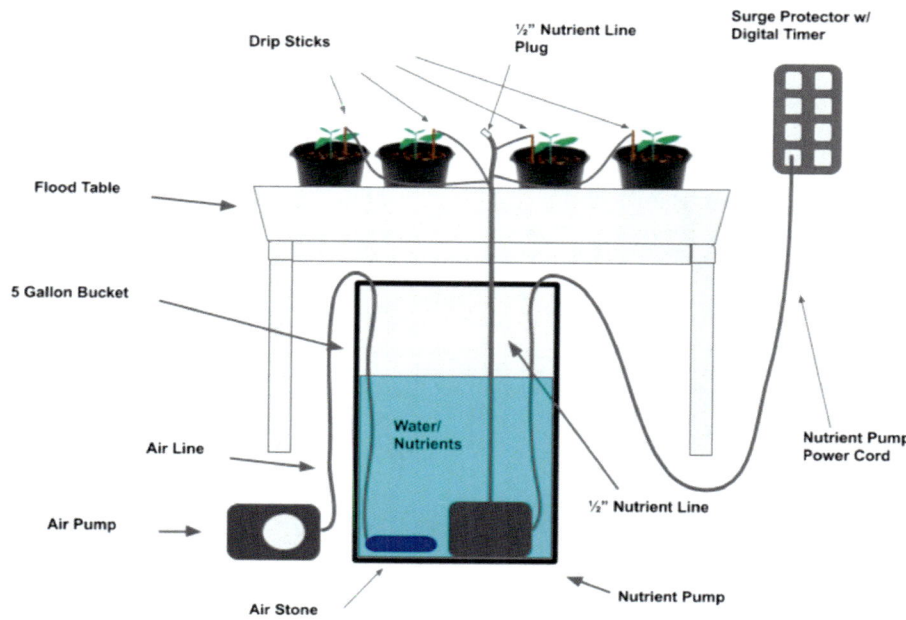

Drip Fed Irrigation System (Top View w/ Parts List)

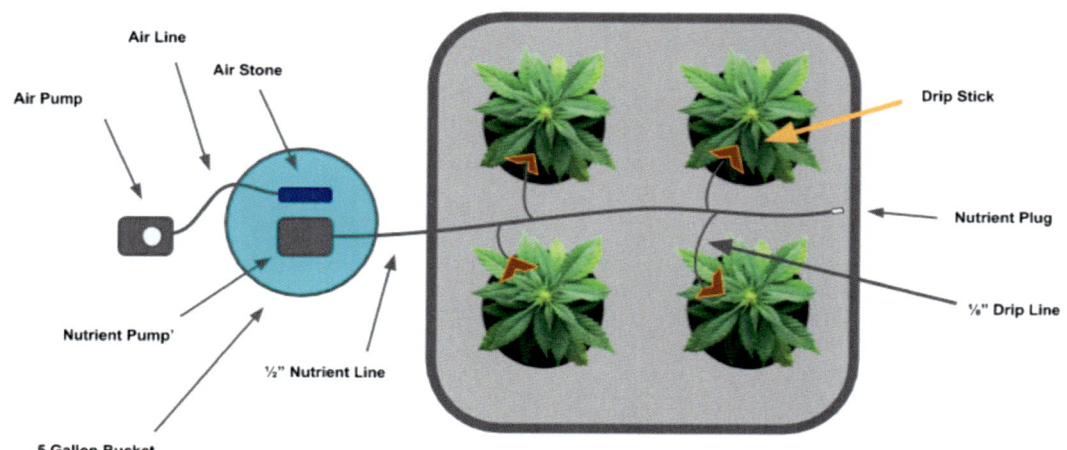

Complete Tent Setup (Top & Side View)

W/ Drip Fed Irrigation

Top View of 4x4 Tent w/ Plants

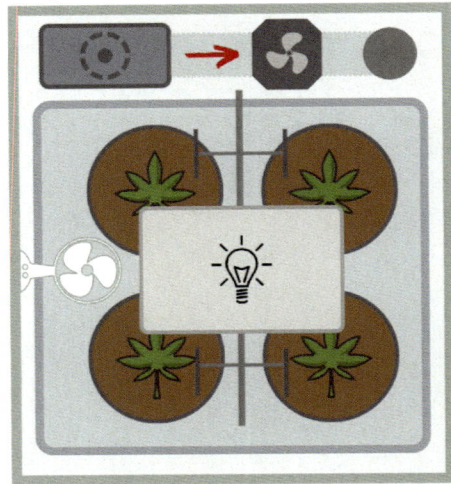

Side View of 4x4 Tent

This tent has a drip fed irrigation system.
See Drip Fed Irrigation Section

ProTip: LED's will reduce the cost of venting dramatically, however be aware of cheap knock-offs.

Vegetative Phase

During this phase we will be training our plants and preparing them for proper canopy coverage. Please check your Production Schedule regularly as you will want to know when to Top/Fim and prune your plant. Once we switch the plants to flowering, your plant will no longer have the ability to regenerate and heal itself quite like in the vegattaive phase. This is because the plants will be transferring all their spent energy towards producing giant buds!

NOTE: The length of this stage really depends on the size of the plants you want in your garden. The taller your tent and the more powerful your light, the more room you'll have to play with in this phase.

During this phase your plant can expect to grow 6" - 8" every two weeks.

<u>Keep in mind</u>: *Your plants will nearly double in size during the flower phase.*

Vegetative Environmental Conditions Checklist

1. **LIGHTS ON: 18 Hours**
   Example: 7:00am - 1:00am

2. **LIGHTS OFF: 6 Hours**
   Example: 1:00am - 7:00am

3. **PPFD:** 400-600

4. **SPECTRUM:** Blue

5. **TEMP:** 70-80°F (20-26.6°C)

6. **HUMIDITY:** Lower 5% each week (40-70%)

7. **SOIL AND WATER PH:** 6.5

How to Prune Your Plants

Pruning is important so there is proper airflow between bud sites in order to reduce mold and mildews. Pruning also places the plants focus on generating big beautiful buds.

*Check the **Production Schedule (PAGE #)** to know when to prune your plants.*

1. Low down branches and leaves that receive little to no light.
2. Bud sites that are low on the plants stalks.
3. Leaves that are dying off due to lack of light.

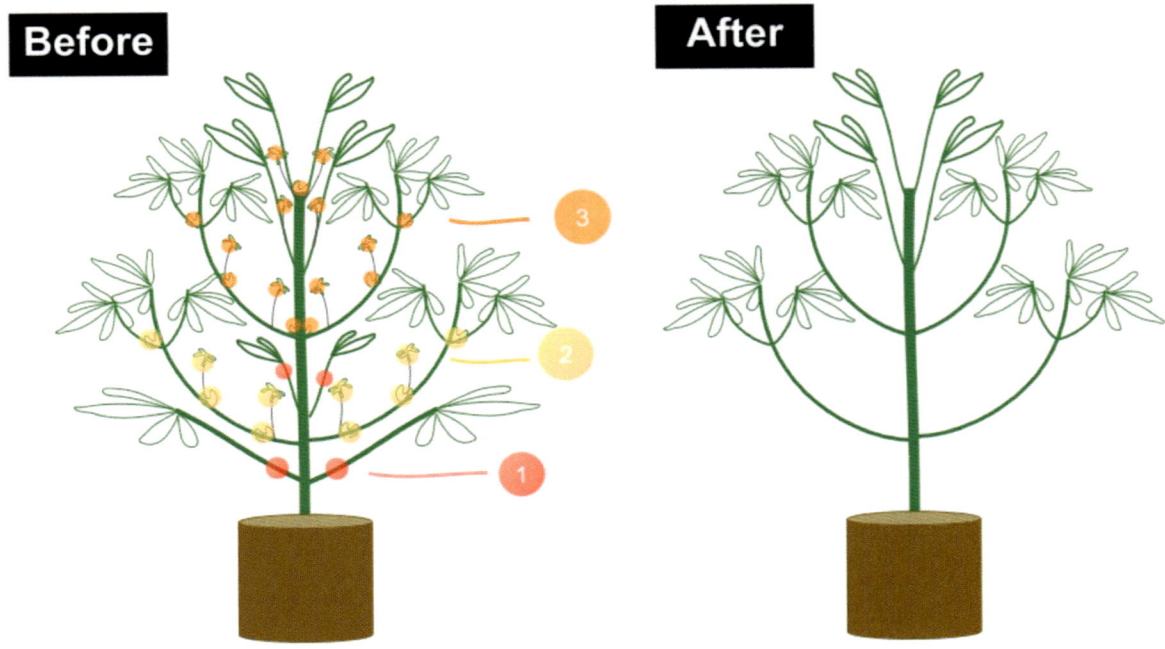

(Shown Above: Prune Illustration. Photo Credits: LearnSativa.org)

How to Top/Fim Your Plants

Topping and Fimming your plant gives you full control over your gardens canopy. These techniques when executed properly will increase your plants yield dramatically when paired with the scrogging technique we will show you later.

(Orange Dots) New branch points creating 4 new cola tops if fimmed at the "Fim Cut Location"

(Red Dots) You will possibly receive new branches in this area. Generally they will form in the shape of a Y when topped at the "Topping Cut Location"

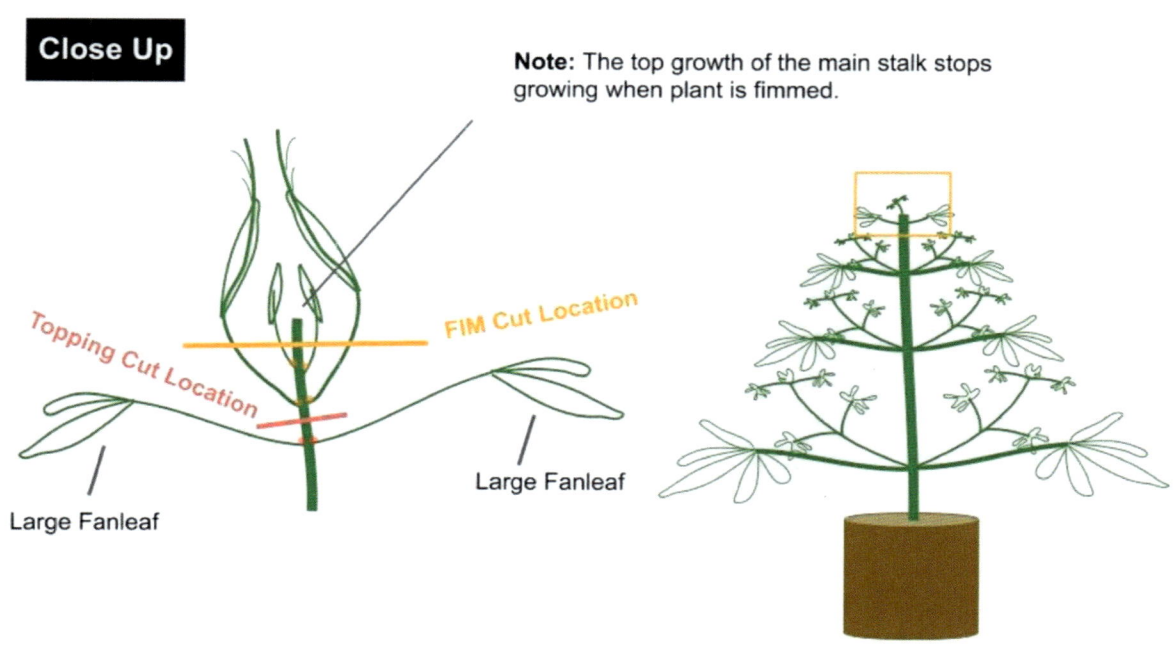

Note: The top growth of the main stalk stops growing when plant is fimmed.

(Shown Above: Topping vs Fimming Illustration. Photo Credits: LearnSativa.org)

How to Scrog Your Garden

The goal to scrogging is to provide your garden with a uniform and even canopy. This technique will also provide you with optimal PPFD coverage and airflow, reducing the risk of mold/mildew when paired with proper ventilation and fans.

(Shown Right: Scrogging Done Right "shown in veg/flower transitioning phase".)

You are basically supporting each cola or growth tip of the plant, so when you enter the flowering phase the buds have some support for the added weight the colas will take on, therefore not damage any of the xylem or cambium aka plants veins if bent or broken.

(Shown Above: Scrogging Done Right "shown in flower phase". Photo Credits: Weedist)

Flower Phase

NOTE: *The length of this stage depends on the strain - typically 8-16 weeks / watch trichomes closely to determine when to harvest.*

During this phase your plants will nearly double in size.

(Shown Right: Scrogging Done Right during Flower Phase. Photo Credits: Cannabis Mag)

Flower Environmental Conditions Checklist

LIGHTS ON: 12 Hours
Example: 7:00am - 7:00am

LIGHTS OFF: 12 Hours
Example: 7:00am - 7:00am

PPFD: 600-900

SPECTRUM: Red

TEMP: 70-78°F (20-26°C) *Lower Temps = Better Oil Production*

HUMIDITY: Lower 5% each week (40-50%)

SOIL AND WATER PH: 6.5

When to Harvest Guide

Harvesting is not that complicated. Simply pay close attention to your trichomes around the time your seed provider tells you to harvest (typically around 12 to 16 weeks).

You can use a jewelers loop or digital USB microscope in order to take a closer look at your plants trichome development.

Your trichomes will go through a series of changes around it's harvesting time. They will initially be clear, then turn cloudy/milking before turning amber.

If you look at the chart below, it will help you know when to harvest your plants in order to get the ideal "vibe" you're looking for.

Be sure to harvest (cut your plants down) before the lights come on in the morning.

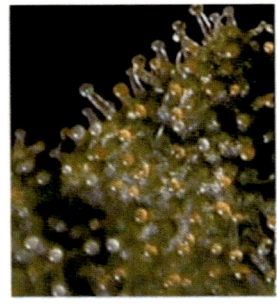

CLEAR	CLOUDY	AMBER	70% CLOUDY 30% AMBER
Not ready for harvest as the plant is not potent enough	Harvesting now will get you an energetic high	Couchlock High Great if your looking to relax	This will proivde you with a very balanced high

Drying Guide

We need to begin the drying process immediately after cutting down and harvesting your plants when your trichomes are ripe to your liking.

Typically we suggest keeping the buds on your plant for easy hanging.

Drying and curing your product is what really differentiates mids from top shelf products. *When dried and cured properly you will truly develop your strains taste and aroma. This means your product will be more valuable to a cannabis connoisseur.*

The goal is to dry your cannabis slowly…

Drying Environmental Conditions Checklist

LIGHTS OFF: 24/7 during the 5-7 days of drying

TEMP: 65-75°F (18-24°C)

HUMIDITY: Start high and lower 5% each day (45-55%)

TIME: 5-7 days

Pro Tip: Avoid placing your flower near air vents or directly blowing air on them to reduce uneven drying however **avoid stagnant air.**

After your cannabis has dried for 7-10 days, remove the stalks and stems from the flower and begin to trim the buds before we cure them.

When trimming your bud, simply start by cutting off the sugar leaves and work your way in until you have a clean, uniform bud. **Trimming is an art** and may take some practice.

Curing Guide

Curing Environmental Conditions Checklist

LIGHTS OFF: 24/7 during the 3-4 weeks of curing

TEMP: 70°F (21.1°C)

HUMIDITY: 62-64%

TIME: 3-4 weeks minimum

BURPING:
First Week = *15/30min Twice a Day*
Second Week = *15/30min Once a Day*
Third Week = *15/30min Every 2-3 Days*

Pro Tip: Use black or UV protectant mason jars to cure & the longer you cure the better your bud will smell and taste.

Moisture Packs: If you'd like some assistance with the humidity, be sure to throw a moisture pack in your jar..

Definition of Burping: Opening jars periodically.

If you notice any moisture developing, open the jar and replace it before burping bud in new jar for about 6 hours.

Mold Prevention Tips: Allow your jars to get fresh air daily and move around the bud gently. Moving around the air prevents mold from forming.

Automated Dry and Cure Machine

Drying and curing can be a hassle, especially when you get to the commercial level. We have a few workarounds however.

In full disclosure, we've never tried using these automated drying/curing systems at a caregiver level and to be completely honest, the price can be a little discouraging at $2,997 (entry level).

However, if you are not afraid of the price and do some research on the reviews, you may come to find that an automated drying / curing solution like the one above may save you some time and headache.

(Shown Above: Commercial Cannabis Curing Room.)

Commonly Asked Grow Questions

Q. When do I water my plants?

A. You always water your plants when the lights come on, never when they go out to avoid mold and mildew issues. Ideally we want to keep the soil moist, not dry or wet (see Soil Moisture Tool).

Q. How much do I water my plants?

A. We recommend turning on your drip fed irrigation system and taking note of the time it takes for your pump to kick on in your reservoir and begin to feed all of your plants water. The moment you seed water coming out of the bottom of your soil pots - **STOP!**

Then take note of the time that entire process took.

For example: Let's say it took 1 min, 45 seconds total to water your entire garden using your drip fed irrigation system: I would then set my digital timer to turn on for 1 min, 45 seconds every morning, as soon as my lights came on.

The Ultimate Cannabis Education Handbook

The Green Print

The Sativa Certification Program

BONUS MATERIAL 100% FREE

How to Grow Guide

https://learnsativa.org/how-to-grow-marijuana

Cannabis Recipes

https://learnsativa.org/edibles

Cannabis Laws for By State

https://learnsativa.org/marijuana-laws-by-state

Cannabis Stocks

https://learnsativa.org/marijuana-stocks

Cannabis Jobs Now Hiring By State

https://learnsativa.org/marijuana-jobs

Find Cannabis Near You

https://learnsativa.org/finder

Dosage Calculator

https://learnsativa.org/cbd-dosage-calculator

Are You Looking for Cannabis?

Try our new, 100% FREE Cannabis Finder Online

Over 10,000+ Legal Cannabis Dispensaries, Doctors, Lawyers, & CBD Companies in All Cannabis Friendly States.

Save Big with Exclusive Coupons & Read Customer Reviews!

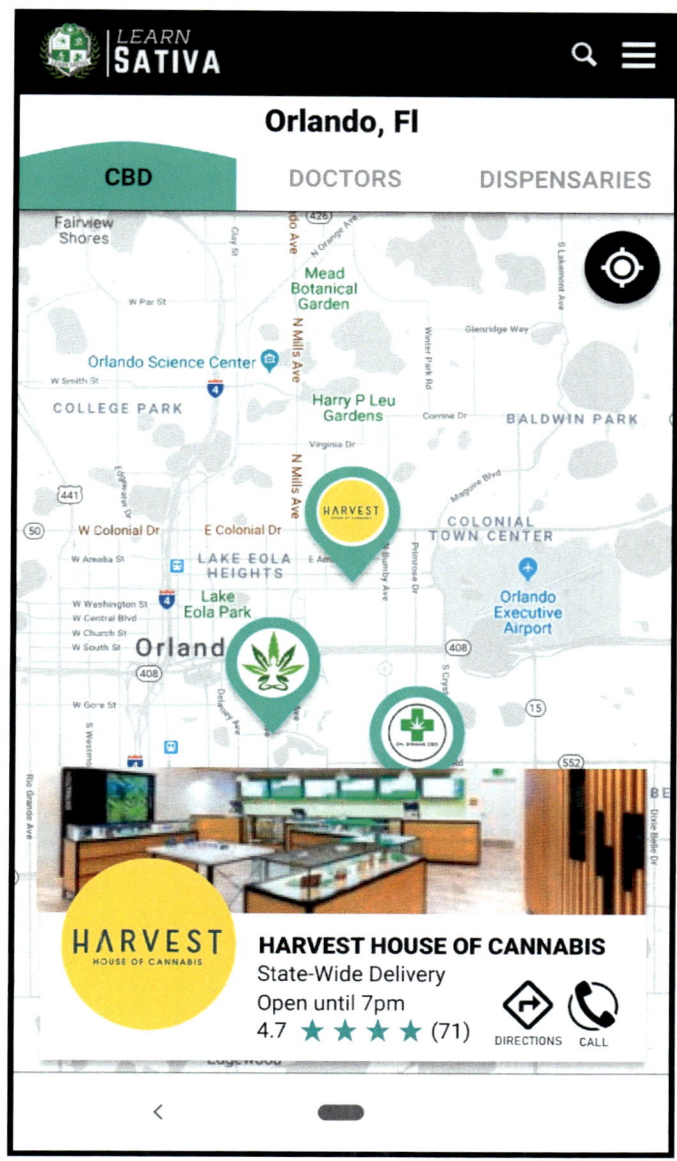

Made in the USA
Middletown, DE
14 November 2025

21533332R00100